# *The Makers*

of MODERN

# RHODE ISLAND

# The Makers

## *of* MODERN
# RHODE ISLAND

PATRICK T. CONLEY

Charleston | London

THE
History
PRESS

Published by The History Press
Charleston, SC 29403
www.historypress.net

Copyright © 2012 by Patrick T. Conley
All rights reserved

*Cover image*: Slater Mill. *Photo courtesy of the National Park Service.*

First published 2012

Manufactured in the United States

ISBN 978.1.60949.164.2

Library of Congress CIP data applied for.

*To*

Dr. Hilliard Beller

*My meticulous editor*
*and*
*the dutiful editor for the*
*Rhode Island Publications Society*
*for more than a third of a century*

# CONTENTS

# CONTENTS

CONTENTS

George Bancroft * Reverend William Ellery Channing * Dr. Walter Channing * Prudence Crandall * John DeWolf * Charles Bird King * Captain Albert Martin * Clement Clarke Moore * Sam Patch * Commodore Oliver Hazard Perry * Commodore Matthew Calbraith Perry * U.S. Minister and Congressman Jonathan Russell * Gilbert Stuart * Judah Touro * Dr. Benjamin Waterhouse * Henry Wheaton

# PREFACE

This volume is a sequel to my earlier History Press volume, *Rhode Island's Founders* (2010), and follows a similar format. When this biographical project was originally conceived in 2008, I had envisioned a book that would span the years from settlement to the Dorr Rebellion, Rhode Island's great constitutional, political and enthnocultural divide. However, the publisher's directive, with its readers in mind, wisely limited the size of that volume (and this). The result is a two-volume set that extends to 1860. In many American history texts, that year is used as the line of demarcation between the antebellum era and the America that emerged from the crucible of the Civil War.

For this book, that dichotomy has only limited relevancy because the characteristics of modern Rhode Island—urban, industrial and ethnoculturally diverse—were established without the impetus of civil war (at least the one fought from 1861 to 1865).

Historian Peter S. Coleman best described the changing nature of the state from agrarian and commercial to urban and industrial in his 1962 book, *The Transformation of Rhode Island, 1790–1860*. I am merely providing profiles of the people who engineered that transformation: those who made Rhode Island the most industrialized American state; those who finally gave it a written constitution and its present structure of government; those who established a comprehensive system of public education; those who fought successfully for social change; those who brought (with great opposition) religious and ethnic diversity; and those whose abilities or exploits— legal, medical, artistic, literary, architectural, philanthropic or spiritual— influenced the state's modern metamorphosis.

By far the most difficult problem in writing this book, apart from its space limitations, was to decide which members of the Rhode Island Heritage Hall of Fame to include as "makers" within my arbitrary (but defensible) time frame: 1790 to 1860. Many of those included herein lived well beyond that terminal date, while other Hall of Fame inductees who predeceased them have been omitted. My basic criterion for selection herein was that the person's major business enterprise; literary, architectural or artistic achievement; reform effort; medical breakthrough; or principal political position was achieved, in full swing or launched during the time frame I have chosen. Those who missed the cut, such as Congressman Thomas Allen Jenckes (the "father of civil service reform"); William T. Nicholson (founder of Nicholson File Company in 1864, one of Providence's five "industrial wonders"); the amazingly versatile and accomplished Providence civic leader Amos Chafee Barstow; textile magnates Benjamin and Robert Knight (who expanded their company dramatically in the late nineteenth century); public health pioneer Dr. Edwin Snow; historian Samuel Greene Arnold; and pioneer black artists Edward and Christiana Bannister are Hall of Fame inductees who will find their way into a sequel to this book, if I live long enough to write one. Other inductees who lived well into the nineteenth century, such as Moses Brown, Senator Theodore Foster and Signer William Ellery, were already profiled in *Founders* because of their efforts in achieving independence and statehood for Rhode Island.

The reader will note that the fifty-six biographical profiles to follow, like encyclopedia entries, are uneven in length. Most notable in the treatment of Thomas Dorr, this disparity is due mainly to the desire to give space to Hall of Fame inductees in proportion to their influence on Rhode Island or the nation. National figures whose exploits were conducted mainly in Rhode Island receive fuller profiles than purely local personalities. Other factors affecting length of treatment might include the multidimensional nature of the subject, the length of his or her productive career, the duration of time spent in Rhode Island or, simply, the amount of information available on the inductee's life.

Though not obsessive-compulsive, I do value structure and symmetry; therefore, I have attempted to impose a semblance of order on this biographical book. My method has been to categorize the biographies using a person's principal occupation or salient feature. Since many Hall of Famers were multidimensional—my hero, Thomas Dorr, was not only a reformer but also a lawyer, politico and educator—these categories are both flexible and fluid. All of my philanthropists were also entrepreneurs (the accumulation of wealth through business endeavor was the source of their enduring generosity), and most of the lawyers herein had an affinity for politics, as did those I have styled reformers.

Since this book is a project of the Rhode Island Heritage Hall of Fame, all fifty-six men and women profiled here have one thing in common: they have earned induction into that pantheon of eminent Rhode Islanders. As I stated in *Rhode Island's Founders*, those eligible for Hall of Fame membership "include those who are native-born, those whose reputations have been made while residents of the state, and those [born elsewhere] who have adopted Rhode Island as their permanent home." The early induction citations for such individuals concluded with the phrase "for your contributions to your community, state, and nation," suggesting that mere fame, wealth or power without civic virtue (or, at least, the absence of wrongful conduct) would not merit selection. This standard, established not by me but by the board of directors when the hall was created in 1965, continues to guide the selection process that I have inherited as Hall of Fame president.

Accordingly, some very prominent and influential figures from this era have been denied entry to the state's Hall of Fame (and to these pages), despite their obvious talent and importance, because they have shaped Rhode Island in ways more negative than positive. In this category are two United States senators—the relentless Bristol slave trafficker James DeWolf (despite his wealth, political power and amazing success as a War of 1812 privateer) and arch-nativist and religious bigot Henry Bowen Anthony (despite his influential publishing career at the *Providence Journal*, his governorship and his leading role in the foundation of the state's Republican Party). Also omitted is the intolerant and injudicious Chief Justice Job Durfee, who lacked the patience of his biblical namesake as he presided with astounding partiality over the trials of Thomas Dorr and John Gordon.

Another sixteen members of the Rhode Island Hall of Fame of national note—some far more famous than most of those included in this volume—are listed in the appendix with a very short biographical profile. Their greatness was achieved beyond the tiny confines of the state and had little direct impact on the making of modern Rhode Island other than to instill in its residents a sense of pride and admiration. This was especially true of naval hero Oliver Hazard Perry, naval officer and diplomat Matthew Calbraith Perry, historian George Bancroft, artist Gilbert Stuart, religious leader William Ellery Channing and daredevil jumper Sam Patch.

In writing this biographical book, spanning about four generations of Rhode Island history through the early national and antebellum eras, certain commonalities made an impression. One was the amount of interaction (and, sometimes, intermarriage) among the leading "makers" of our micro paradise, despite their diverse talents and vocations. Another was the longevity of those profiled (some of whom lived into the early twentieth century). This characteristic was not common among the wives of the male achievers. They often bore many, many children (Bishop Griswold had fourteen, John Howland had thirteen, Wilkins Updike had twelve, Philip Allen had eleven and Sam Slater and Dr. Solomon Drowne each had nine), and the complications of childbirth made many husbands widowers early in the marriage. Those who ventured into the business world often achieved success by risk-taking, which also led to bankruptcy. Economic reversals (especially those suffered by John Holden Greene, David Wilkinson, John Gorham and the Spragues) were devastating to their careers, but their Hall of Fame status supports the maxim: "No pain, no gain." And whereas Newport dominated colonial Rhode Island, Providence had emerged as the state's undisputed leader by 1860. Despite the fact that it was then less than one-third its present area (Providence was enlarged by several post–Civil War annexations from Cranston, North Providence and Johnston), the city in 1860 had 29 percent of the state's population (50,666 out of 174,620), and most of the "makers" (with the Hazards a notable exception) made their mark in this emerging metropolis, even though they may have resided elsewhere.

When I once taught a graduate course in historical methodology, I warned my students about "presentism" (judging historical characters by the standards of today) and about imposing an artificial pattern on the past that would have been unrecognizable to those who lived it. Hopefully, the Hall of Fame's exclusion of men like James DeWolf, Henry Anthony and Job Durfee, and my own arbitrary categories, do not blatantly violate those precepts.

As I also stated in the introduction to *Founders*, it is hoped that the profiles contained herein will provide present-day Rhode Islanders with illustrious models to admire and to inspire. For a state that had only one-fifty-seventh of the population of the United States in 1790 and proportionally less in each year thereafter, the achievements recited here should generate not only a wellspring of local pride but even a gusher.

# Acknowledgements

L ike all of my recent books, this one is due largely to the efforts of Anna Maria Loiselle and Linda Gallen, my nimble-fingered secretaries, and Dr. Hilliard Beller, the meticulous editor of the Rhode Island Publications Society, to whom this book is dedicated.

Photographer Frank Mullen provided the illustrations, and the Rhode Island Heritage Hall of Fame furnished funding for the photography and copyediting, as well as permissions for most of the portrait photos in this volume.

Certain historians have developed an expertise concerning one or more of our "makers." I have asked them to read and critique my biographical sketches as they pertain to their person or persons of interest. These scholars and their subjects are as follows: Rick Greenwood of the Rhode Island Historical Preservation and Heritage Commission (John Holden Greene, Russell Warren, James C. Bucklin and Thomas A. Tefft); South County historian Christian McBurney, Esq. (Elisha R. Potter Jr., Wilkins Updike, Thomas R. Hazard and Rowland Gibson Hazard); Dr. Scott Molloy, founder of the Rhode Island Labor History Society (Seth Luther); Kevin Klyberg, park ranger, Blackstone Valley National Heritage Corridor (Samuel Slater and David Wilkinson); William Vareika, proprietor of the Vareika Art Gallery (James Sullivan Lincoln); Nathanael Greene Herreshoff (Bishop Alexander Viets Griswold); Russell DeSimone, past president of the Bartlett Society (John Russell Bartlett); the Reverend Dr. Robert Hayman, historian of the Diocese of Providence (Father James Fitton and Mother Frances Xavier Warde); Paul Campbell, Providence city archivist (Nehemiah Dodge, Jabez Gorham, John Gorham and Ebenezer Knight Dexter); and Dr. Elizabeth Stevens, editor of *Rhode Island History* (Arnold Buffum and

Elizabeth Buffum Chace). Their expertise has given greater precision to my profiles. Al Klyberg, my longtime associate in promoting the study of our state's history and the director emeritus of the Rhode Island Historical Society, read the manuscript in its entirety and offered valuable suggestions.

Finally, I am grateful to The History Press, not only for furthering this project of the Rhode Island Heritage Hall of Fame but also for publishing local history that enlightens the general reader while enriching our knowledge of the past.

# I

# THE ENTREPRENEURS

## SAMUEL SLATER

Samuel Slater, more than any single person, pioneered the making of modern Rhode Island. This so-called Father of the Factory System was the catalyst for the economic transformation that gave Rhode Island its salient characteristic—an industrial order that dominated the state's economy from the early nineteenth century until the dawn of the present postindustrial era. Slater, with his brother, John, also established the iconic Rhode Island factory mill village of Slatersville that became a model for industrial villages nationwide. Large-scale local manufacturing, jumpstarted by Slater, spawned urbanization and attracted an immigrant workforce that eventually became ethnoculturally and religiously diverse.

Slater himself was an immigrant. He was born in 1768 in Belper, a Derbyshire town in the north-central area of England. He was the fifth child of eight in a farm family presided over by his father, William, and his mother, the former Elizabeth Fox. At the age of ten, he began work at a cotton mill owned by Jedidiah Strutt on the Derwent River, a facility that utilized a water frame pioneered by Strutt's partner, Richard Arkwright. On January 6, 1783, after the death of his father in a farming accident, Samuel became formally apprenticed to Strutt, from whom he gained a thorough knowledge of Arkwright's revolutionary water-powered machinery and where he had a role in supervising the erection of one of Arkwright's new factories in the Derwent Valley.

In 1789, as Slater observed his twenty-first birthday and his indenture to Strutt ended, this ambitious and technically proficient young man sought

Samuel Slater.

to leave the laboring class and become a textile entrepreneur. America, rather than stratified England, provided this opportunity. Also in 1789, the U.S. Congress passed its first act for the encouragement of manufacturers, and Pennsylvania offered a bounty to "which man will bring us English models [of textile production]." Despite the legal ban against exporting such technology from England, including a heavy fine and twelve months' imprisonment, Slater thoroughly grasped both the plans for Arkwright's machinery and Strutt's managerial practices and defiantly set out for America on September 13, 1789, allegedly disguised as a farmhand. Sixty-six days later, he arrived in New York, where he soon became aware of the activities of Providence merchant Moses Brown, who was attempting to expand his family's manufacturing business from iron and candles to include cotton textiles.

In partnership with his cousin Smith Brown and his son-in-law William Almy, Moses Brown had acquired a former fulling mill in 1789 at Pawtucket Falls, the last drop of the Blackstone River on its course to Narragansett Bay. In August of that year, this trio had also purchased a thirty-two-spindle frame, but its operation proved unsuccessful in making yarn sufficiently strong to be used by their looms. In late 1789, news of Moses Brown's incipient venture reached the recently arrived Slater via the captain of a costal packet from Providence. On December 2, Slater wrote to Brown to offer his expertise. In this missive, he expressed his intention "to erect a perpetual card and spinning" machine, a code phrase that indicated that Slater could reproduce the Arkwright patents. Brown immediately responded that he was "destitute of a person acquainted with water-frame spinning" and thus was prepared to make Slater a generous business offer "to come and work ours, and have the credit as well as the advantage of perfecting the first water-mill in America."

Slater responded eagerly, and he arrived in the North Providence village of Pawtucket within a month. Here he discovered a heterogeneous collection of ill-made machines that he found of little use, so Slater and several woodworkers and mechanics, including Sylvanus Brown, Plinney Earl, Oziel Wilkinson and David Wilkinson, along with the help of black laborer and former slave Samuel Primus, constructed machinery based on the Arkwright plans. Slater, who stood over six feet in height and weighed well over two hundred pounds, did some of the arduous work.

In April 1790, with some of the reconstruction completed, Moses Brown withdrew from the business and prepared a three-way partnership agreement for his son, Almy and Slater, giving Slater a one-half interest in the venture. All work on the revamped project was completed by the autumn of 1790. After some discouraging failed attempts, the three eighteen-inch carding machines and a complex array of drawing and roving machines, winders and two spinning frames with a total of seventy-two spindles began to operate in harmony, with nine children working the frames. On that day, December 20, 1790, cotton yarn was spun by water power for the first time in America.

Secretary of the Treasury Alexander Hamilton cited Slater's mill in his famous 1791 *Report on Manufacturers*, wherein he observed that "the manufactory at Providence has the merit of being the first in introducing into the United States the celebrated cotton mill; which not only furnishes materials for the manufactory itself, but for the supply of private families for household manufacture." Gradually, almost imperceptibly at first, from this achievement Rhode Island began a metamorphosis away from its agricultural and maritime economy that would alter not only its economic but also its political, constitutional and social complexion.

Slater taught his partners how to manage the business profitably by efficiently coordinating materials, machines, labor and record keeping, using the techniques taught to him by Arkwright and Strutt. According to some economic historians, these management procedures were at least as important to the success of this venture as was Slater's technical knowledge and skill.

Slater's management and organizational style, called "the Rhode Island System," drew on his English experience, as did the decision of this devout Episcopalian to employ young boys and to establish Sunday school Bible classes for them at Pawtucket and in his other mill villages. These Sunday schools for his youthful workers were the first of their kind in America.

Paternalistic child labor was not frowned upon in Slater's time, even by such pious Quakers as Moses Brown and Oziel Wilkinson. Because children were already accustomed to rigorous farm work, the mills simply continued a long-standing attitude that children should help their families if they could.

The poor children recruited by Slater usually enhanced the economic status of both Slater and their own families.

In 1793, Slater and Sylvanus Brown built a new, larger mill nearby, more suited to their expanding operations. Today, that surviving structure, called Old Slater Mill, is the centerpiece of the Slater Mill National Historic Site. Five years later, Slater split from Almy and Brown and formed Samuel Slater and Company in partnership with his father-in-law, Oziel Wilkinson. That enterprise eventually developed additional mills, initially in Massachusetts (the first of which was the so-called White Mill just across the Blackstone River in what was then Rehoboth).

A brief profile such as this does not permit a detailed discussion of labor relations, working conditions, technical innovations, marketing, financial machinations or changing business associations among Slater's various factories. One of the most important developments in his expanding empire, however, was the arrival of his younger brother John, who emigrated from Derbyshire in 1803, bringing with him information about the new spinning mule and other more recent technical developments in this cradle of the English textile industry. Working again with Almy and Brown, Samuel and John established the first planned industrial village in the United States on the Branch River in present-day North Smithfield, Rhode Island. They proudly called their creation Slatersville. By 1813, this model mill village contained 5,170 spindles, the largest aggregation on any site in America.

Over the next two decades, Samuel, his sons, his in-laws and his associates opened mills in Wilkinsonville, Oxford, Dudley and Webster, Massachusetts (the latter town was created by Slater); in Jewett City and Hopeville, Connecticut; at Amoskeag Falls, New Hampshire; in the village of Central Falls on the Blackstone River; and in Providence, where he constructed one of the nation's earliest steam-powered mills in 1827. His achievements were so impressive that Presidents James Monroe and Andrew Jackson made visits to Slater at his Pawtucket mill to pay him homage.

Slater's "Rhode Island System" of mill operation relied not only on children and adults from poor rural families but also on a number of young boys from the middle class, who sometimes entered the factory with the aim of gaining the skills to become machinists, managers and even mill owners. Slater-trained mechanics spread his technology throughout the Blackstone Valley and beyond.

Slater's system was also characterized by on-site management by an owner-partner, a village setting and limited capitalization. It differed from the pattern known as the Waltham System, later developed by Francis Cabot

Lowell, that preferred as employees young middle-class women living in chaperoned dormitories, used the corporate form of business organization to become highly capitalized, was usually city-based and emphasized integrated mass production from cotton to cloth.

The Wilkinson family of Pawtucket helped Slater in a variety of ways, not the least of which was to furnish him a wife. In 1791, he married Hannah Wilkinson, who bore him nine children; together, the couple would raise six boys, with one other son and two daughters dying in infancy. Shortly after their marriage, Hannah invented a type of cotton sewing thread, superior to the customary linen fiber, an innovation that enabled her to become, in 1793, the first American woman to be granted a patent.

Five years after Hannah's death from consumption in 1812, Samuel married Esther Parkinson, the widow of a friend. They had no children. Esther and others have left assessments of Slater that were distilled into an estimate of his character by the writers of the commemorative volume *The Cotton Centennial, 1790–1890*: "In manner he was quiet, unassuming, and modest; in character honest, conscientious, and of the strictest integrity; in conduct exact, punctual, decisive, with indomitable perseverance and energy." Samuel Slater had a commanding presence.

After business reversals in an 1829 financial panic, Slater rebounded, largely because of the intervention of Moses Brown. Despite declining health caused by digestive ailments, by 1835 Slater had founded, purchased or partially owned sixteen firms, thirteen of which were textile mills, and he was the founding director of Pawtucket's Slater Bank. Then, at age sixty-six, he died at home in his mill village of Webster, Massachusetts, where he was laid to rest. Samuel Slater left to his surviving wife and family an estate that far exceeded $1 million and to Rhode Island and America an industrial legacy that has shaped their histories.

# DAVID WILKINSON

When a historical movement is particularly successful, it is logical that there would be many claims of authorship. This is certainly true of the Industrial Revolution and the beginnings of the American factory system. At the center of the Industrial Revolution's story is, of course, Samuel Slater, but it does not detract from Slater's reputation to add more personalities to the story. Of all the possible additions, none is more appropriate and worthy of inclusion than David Wilkinson.

David Wilkinson.

David was born near the village of Manville in what was then the town of Smithfield, Rhode Island, on January 5, 1771, into a Quaker family headed by locally renowned and greatly talented blacksmith and metalworker Oziel Wilkinson. David was one of five sons, all raised in the metals trade. In the early 1780s, Oziel moved his large family, consisting of his wife, Lydia, and four daughters, to the North Providence village of Pawtucket at the final falls of the Blackstone River. Here they settled on a small road called Quaker Lane.

At first, Oziel began making anchors for Providence merchants. Then, Moses Brown enlisted him to fabricate machinery for a proposed cotton mill at Pawtucket Falls. As this venture floundered, Brown recruited Samuel Slater, just off the boat from England, to construct an Arkwright water-powered spinning system. Oziel and nineteen-year-old David contributed mightily to this enterprise, and they then became associates of Brown and Slater in various industrial enterprises. In 1791, David acquired Slater as a brother-in-law when the English immigrant married his sister Hannah.

David Wilkinson was a mechanical genius and a self-taught mechanical engineer. Among his early ventures was a steamboat. In 1803, Robert Fulton made transportation history when his steamboat, the *Clermont*, churned up the Hudson River. However, a decade before this heralded event, David French, one of Fulton's draftsmen, had visited Rhode Island to examine a boat aptly named the *Experiment*. This twelve-ton ferry had been built in 1792 by Elijah Ormsbee, a Providence carpenter, and it contained a steam engine crafted by David Wilkinson. These two young men presented tickets for contemplated trips from Providence to Newport on their ferry. With spectators lining the banks of the Seekonk River—an extension of the

Blackstone below Pawtucket Falls—the duo navigated the *Experiment* from Providence northward to Pawtucket "between the bridges." According to Wilkinson's later reminiscences, the boat was propelled by a "goose foot paddle" instead of a side wheel. After the "frolic," as Wilkinson called it, the boat was "hauled up," and for some unexplained reason, this promising venture was abandoned. So Fulton got the credit for the first successful steamboat.

David Wilkinson's projects with Slater and Ormsbee were only the beginning of a remarkable career. From childhood, he possessed an observant and practical mind. What seemed trifles to most were to him the germ of some remarkable invention. In a letter describing his invention of a new machine for cutting screws using a gauge and sliding lathe, begun in 1794 and perfected in 1797, he states that

> *the perfection of it consists in that most faithful agent,* gravity, *making the joint, and that almighty perfect number,* three, *which is harmony itself. I was young when I learned that principle. I had never seen my grandmother putting a chip under a three-legged milking-stool; but she always had to put a chip under a four-legged stool to keep it steady.* [Using this insight], *I cut screws of all dimensions with the machine and did them perfectly. As one historian of technology has stated, "Too great an importance cannot be given to the slide lathe—that is to say, speaking technically, the slide rest and its combination with the lead screw, operated by change gears—because this combination is used in some form in almost every machine tool…the machines to make machines, without which machine building on a large scale would have been impossible."*

Wilkinson's contribution was the ability of his machine to trace precisely the model part to be reproduced. He obtained a patent for his invention in 1798, but very little profit had accrued to him before the patent expired. Because of his preoccupation with other ventures, he failed to renew it.

Wilkinson expanded his business efforts to include partnerships in textile mills, but his main focus was the creation of machinery to be used in those mills and metalwork for a variety of purposes. At the turn of the century, David and his brother Daniel established an iron manufactory in Pawtucket known as David Wilkinson & Company. Here, David produced cannons in the furnace that were cast solid and then bored out using water power by making the drill or bore stationary and having the cannon revolve around the drill. Some claim that this innovation produced the world's first solid-cast cannon.

During the first decade of the nineteenth century, the Wilkinsons' machine business was so brisk that Oziel and David built a three-and-a-half-story factory in 1810 close to Slater Mill. That structure is now restored, operating and an integral part of the Slater Mill Historic Site, along with the Sylvanus Brown House, occupied by the man who assisted Wilkinson in the development of the slide lathe. Originally, the upper floors of the Wilkinson Mill were used for cotton spinning, with a machine shop run by David occupying the first floor, where David had built a steam engine that supplemented the mill's water-power capacity. According to some historians of technology, this innovation made this factory the first steam-powered mill in Rhode Island and one of the first in the nation.

After expanding his business in 1813 by moving to a large building, constructed by Eleazer Jenks on the south side of Main Street in Pawtucket, Wilkinson built the most successful early American power loom. He accomplished this feat in 1817 from patterns supplied by the Scottish inventor William Gilmour, not in Pawtucket but in the North Providence village of Lymansville, as requested by mill owner Daniel Lyman. Then, in 1819, working with English immigrant William Wilson Wood, David began the production of worsted yarn on a seventy-two-spindle frame above his Pawtucket machine shop, making this mill one of the first worsted manufactories in the United States.

From 1811 to 1829, according to Wilkinson's own account, his factory made and shipped textile machinery to dozens of mills in southern New England, throughout the Middle Atlantic states, as far west as Pittsburgh and as far south as Georgia and Louisiana. "Indeed," as Wilkinson exclaimed, "Pawtucket was doing something for almost every part of the country!"

During this time, Wilkinson continued his business relationship with his brother-in-law Sam Slater in the cotton textile industry. One of their joint ventures resulted in the establishment of a mill village on the Blackstone River in the northeastern sector of the Massachusetts town of Sutton, which he named Wilkinsonville in honor of his family.

Then came the financial panic of 1829, a downturn that crippled Samuel Slater temporarily, but one that ruined David Wilkinson, despite Slater's efforts to assist him. After Wilkinson's business failed, he moved to Cohoes, New York, near Albany, where he became one of the original directors of a firm organized to develop power from Cohoes Falls on the Mohawk River. In 1831, Wilkinson and his brother-in-law Hezekiah Howe, who had been his business associate in Pawtucket and Wilkinsonville, established a cotton mill in Cohoes. Though Wilkinson retained his interest in this venture, he moved on to provide expertise in the construction of canal locks and bridges in New York, New Jersey, Ohio and Canada.

David Wilkinson never regained his pre-1829 financial status, but he did receive a bonanza in 1848, when the U.S. Congress voted to award him the handsome sum of $10,000 as a partial recompense for his invention of the gauge and sliding lathe, no longer protected by the 1798 patent that Wilkinson had neglected to renew. This award acknowledged that his device was then in use in all governmental workshops and arsenals and in hundreds of private establishments. The Senate committee that recommended the appropriation called Wilkinson's brainchild "a most powerful and striking illustration of the force of American genius."

It would not be an exaggeration to dub David Wilkinson "the munificent mechanic." This Quaker convert to Episcopalianism donated some Pawtucket land in 1828 as a site for St. Mary's Church, the first structure built as a Catholic church in Rhode Island. According to one account, "He gave the land in hopes of satisfying the spiritual needs of his employees." He was also instrumental in establishing such Episcopalian houses of worship as St. Paul's in Pawtucket, St. John's in Wilkinsonville, St. John's in Cohoes and a chapel in Caledonia Springs, Ontario, Canada, where he died on February 3, 1852, at the age of eighty-one.

Wilkinson's devoted wife, by whom he had four children, was Martha Sayles, a direct descendant of Roger Williams. She died two days before David, and both were returned home to Pawtucket for final burial.

This paramount example of Yankee ingenuity trained many of America's first generation of professional machine builders. David Wilkinson and his talented family were more responsible than any others for the early development of Rhode Island's machine and base metals industry, one of the four cornerstones of nineteenth-century Rhode Island's industrial might.

# EDWARD CARRINGTON

The transition of Rhode Island from an agricultural and maritime economy into one based on industrial production is no better illustrated than in the careers of Providence merchant-industrialists Nicholas Brown and Edward Carrington. Carrington was born in New Haven, Connecticut, on November 2, 1775, the son of physician Edward Carrington and the former Susan Whittlesey. His family moved to Providence after the Revolution, and here Edward embarked on a career in maritime commerce.

Edward Carrington.

The exotic China and East India trade from the port of Providence began in December 1787, when John Brown and his son-in-law John Francis sent their ship *General Washington* to China with rum, cheese, spermaceti candles and cannons from the Scituate factory at Hope Furnace. The ship returned on July 2, 1789, laden with tea, gunpowder (a product the Chinese invented), silk, flannel, chinaware dishes and a small fortune in profit for its sponsors. When he reached his majority, Carrington zealously embraced this commercial opportunity. In 1802, after serving as a clerk for three local merchants, he went to Canton, China, to facilitate trade, and he soon was appointed United States consul, a position he held until 1811. In that capacity, he represented the interests of other American merchants, and he often challenged the English practice of impressing American seamen (a form of kidnapping using the excuse that these sailors were really British runaways), an abuse that became a cause of the War of 1812.

At the conclusion of the second war with England, a conflict that stifled American shipping, Carrington established the commercial firm of Edward Carrington & Company in partnership with Samuel Wetmore of Middletown, Connecticut. This firm enjoyed phenomenal growth. It built numerous ships and at one time owned twenty-six merchantmen engaged in global commerce—Providence's largest fleet.

Using profits derived from trade with the Orient, Europe, South America and Africa, Carrington became a principal promoter, with Nicholas Brown and Thomas P. Ives, of the Blackstone Canal between Providence and Worcester, a public works project designed to bring the produce of the Blackstone Valley southward to the port of Providence while sending raw cotton in bales north to new mills. Begun in 1824, with a large contingent of Irish immigrant laborers, it opened on October 7, 1828, when the *Lady Carrington*, named for Edward's wife, Loriana, arrived in Worcester, making this barge the first boat to traverse the full length of the canal. In that same year, Carrington built the Hamlet Mill in present-day Woonsocket. He followed this venture into the cotton textile industry by building the Carrington Mill (also called Clinton Mill) nearby in this strategic area along the Blackstone River. Carrington also had an interest in the huge Lonsdale Company (established in 1834) and its cotton mill in the Cumberland village of Ashton, and he helped to finance the construction of a railroad spur from India Point across the Seekonk to connect with the new Boston-to-Providence railroad.

Carrington was very active in political and civic affairs. From 1815 to 1818, he served a stint as brigadier general of the Providence County Brigade of state militia, earning him his favored title of "General." He was also a delegate to Rhode Island's first constitutional convention in 1824, the foreman of a forty-five-member volunteer fire company in Providence (Hydraulion No. 1) and a Whig member of the General Assembly representing Providence. He served on the war council of Law and Order governor Samuel Ward King during the Dorr Rebellion. Ironically, his only son, Edward Jr., had married Candace Dorr, sister of the controversial reformer, on February 22, 1841.

Carrington lived on Williams Street, off Hope Street, on Providence's East Side. He furnished his mansion with oriental rugs, porcelains, furniture, sculpture, paintings, vases and other objects of art, most acquired from the Orient. Many of these items are now owned and displayed by the Rhode Island Historical Society and the Rhode Island School of Design. A huge collection of the Carrington business papers, preserved and donated by Margarethe L. Dwight (Edward Carrington's sole surviving descendant), is now housed at the Rhode Island Historical Society and constitutes one of the nation's great private mercantile archives of the early nineteenth century.

On January 30, 1841, the ship *Lion* became the last East Indiaman (as there vessels were called) to enter the port of Providence, and on December 23 of that year, the *Panther*, destined for Batavia in the Dutch East Indies, became the last to depart from Providence. Edward Carrington owned both ships. Exactly two years to the day after Providence's China trade ended, Carrington's own life ended when he died of stomach cancer at his Providence home while still a member of the General Assembly. The state's leading lawyer, John Whipple, gave the merchant prince a moving eulogy.

## NEHEMIAH DODGE

The production of jewelry and silverware (precious metals) constituted one of the four main areas of industrial endeavor in Rhode Island from the early nineteenth century onward (cotton textiles, woolen textiles and base metals/machinery were the other three). Just as Samuel Slater was the textile pioneer and the Wilkinsons were the catalysts in the development of the metals and machinery business, Nehemiah Dodge and especially his apprentice, Jabez Gorham, were the major initiators of the silverware industry in which Rhode Island would eventually rank first in America and possibly the world.

Silversmith Nehemiah Dodge of Providence, though certainly not the first Rhode Island silversmith of note (no more than the Wilkinsons were the state's first metalworkers), provided the spark and the innovative techniques that transformed a traditional sole-proprietor craft producing for local consumption into a manufacturing enterprise that employed many and distributed widely.

Dodge was born on December 17, 1774, in Pomfret, Connecticut, a small town about thirty-two miles northwest of Providence at the end of

The studio and workshop of Seril and Nehemiah Dodge (shown here) was built in 1791 on Thomas Street, then called Angell's Lane. Since 1886, it has been the home of the Providence Art Club.

the Putnam Pike (now U.S. Route 44). In 1794, at the age of twenty, he set up shop in Providence just north of the First Baptist Church, near Roger Williams Spring. Probably he was attracted to that town by the presence of his half brother, Seril Dodge, an established clock and watch maker since the 1770s who had begun to sell various gold and silver necklaces, bracelets and rings, according to his 1793 advertisement. Actually, it was Seril who locally introduced plated gold—a thin gold or gold alloy foil rolled out and backed with a sixty-forty tin-lead solder. Called French plating in Europe and close plating in England, it became known in America as "soft solder gold." This process formed the basis for costume jewelry production.

Nehemiah worked with Seril in the refinement of this technique, but his drive and marketing skills, and his longevity in this trade, made him more productive and widely known. With Seril's retirement shortly after Nehemiah's arrival in Providence, the younger Dodge rented Seril's studio at 11 Thomas Street on College Hill (now occupied by the Providence Art Club) and took on a succession of partners over the next fifteen years, but no associate had more promise than Jabez Gorham, who became an apprentice to Nehemiah in 1807.

The ambitious Dodge soon began to sell his plated product to other goldsmiths, and thus he became the first "manufacturing jeweler." As such, according to jewelry historians, he instituted two trends that would long continue to characterize the Providence jewelry industry: the production of "costume" jewelry in the lower price range and innovation in the technology of jewelry manufacture.

Rather than utilizing mass production, as occurred in contemporary textile and metals industries (and would later occur in the jewelry and silverware trades, as well), most early costume jewelry firms remained small, used the partnership form of business organization, operated with modest amounts of capital and made little investment in machinery. Aside from foot-treadle lathes and drills, pieces were crafted by hand.

Dodge remained in the business he pioneered throughout his life. By 1850, when he was seventy-six, Providence, with a population of 41,513, had fifty-seven jewelry firms employing 590 workers, many of them women. Most of the shops were in the area of North Main Street. Mass production and the movement of the industry to the so-called Jewelry District due south of Downtown was still in the future, but already Providence led the nation in this area of manufacturing endeavor, far outdistancing Attleboro, Massachusetts, its major rival.

Dodge died in Providence on June 16, 1856, at the age of eighty-one. His wife, Sarah Crawford Tripe, whom he married in 1795, predeceased him. Unfortunately, little is known about Nehemiah's personal life, and no likeness of him has survived, but his local legacy as the "father of costume jewelry manufacturing" is well established and secure.

## JABEZ AND JOHN GORHAM

Unlike the relatively obscure (at least historically) Nehemiah Dodge, Jabez Gorham had deep and prominent New England roots and a public persona apart from his craft. His ancestor Captain John Gorham was Bristol's first settler in the early 1670s, when that area was part of Plymouth Colony and the domain of the Pokanokets. Another relative, Nathaniel Gorham, was president of Congress under the Confederation and a Massachusetts delegate to the Philadelphia Convention of 1787. In contrast to these prominent

Jabez Gorham.

Gorhams, the father of Jabez (also named Jabez) was a Providence harness maker who married Catherine Tyler in 1762. They produced ten children, of whom Jabez, born on February 15, 1792, was the sixth.

After attending the common schools of Providence, Jabez became apprenticed to silversmith Nehemiah Dodge in 1807. With Dodge's guidance, Gorham learned the trade but chose not to emulate his mentor by crafting costume jewelry when he concluded his apprenticeship in 1813. Not long thereafter, Jabez

John Gorham.

entered into a partnership (as was quite common in this business) with other craftsmen and began the manufacture of gold jewelry on the second floor of a building at the corner of North Main and Steeple Street in Providence's original jewelry district. In 1818, after five years of partnership operation, Gorham became the sole proprietor and soon won a regional reputation by making French filigree jewelry and a special kind of popular gold chain that became known as the "Gorham chain." From 1825 through 1840, Jabez took on a succession of three partners—Stanton Beebe, Henry Lamson Webster and William Gladding Price—the latter of whom married Jabez's daughter Amanda. The Webster partnership, which opened a shop at 12 Steeple Street in 1831, made the momentous shift to silver spoons as its leading product. From that point onward, silverware and Gorham became synonymous.

In 1837, Jabez took on an apprentice who would one day transform the Gorham Manufacturing Company into a world leader in the production of silverware, holloware and statuary. That protégée was his third child, John, whose birth on November 18, 1820, caused complications that led to the death of Gorham's first wife, Amey Thurber, eight days later at the age of twenty-five.

In 1839, Jabez withdrew from his partnership with Webster and Price but continued to manufacture his Gorham chain. Meanwhile, other activities had begun to occupy his time. In 1822, he had married Lydia Dexter, who bore him four more children by 1834. In addition to his family responsibilities, Jabez had become a proprietor of the Eagle Screw Company, the captain of a militia unit and a Whig member of the Rhode Island General Assembly. Perhaps at the urging of his son John, he resumed the manufacture of spoons and silverware in 1841 at 12 Steeple Street by forming the firm of J. Gorham & Son. From 1842 to 1844, however, he also found time to serve on the Providence Common Council.

Jabez retired permanently from the business in 1847, having achieved both fame and prosperity. In 1858, he and his wife built an imposing brick house at the corner of Benefit and Bowen Streets, where Jabez continued to reside until his death on March 24, 1869, at the age of seventy-seven.

John Gorham proved to be a most worthy successor to Jabez. His father's business model relied on a small number of craftsmen producing a limited number of quality items, but John quickly began to recognize the advantages of mechanization to augment hand craftsmanship in the production of silverware. His research into manufacturing processes brought him to the Springfield Arsenal in Massachusetts and the U.S. Mint in Philadelphia, where he learned procedures for handling large quantities of coin silver.

His entry into silver manufacturing was blessed by good timing. In 1842, those engaged in the production of silverware successfully petitioned Congress to impose a 30 percent ad valorem tax on imported silver, a levy that gave American manufacturers a major impetus to increase production. After John bought out his father's interest in 1847, his incessant drive to learn more about his competitors and their business practices brought him, in 1852, to Europe, where he visited English factories in Birmingham and Sheffield, the London Mint and the Woolwich Arsenal, as well as silver shops in Brussels and Paris. Upon his return to Providence, Gorham quickly introduced factory methods to augment hand craftsmanship, installed a steam engine to power his new machinery and even designed new machinery himself. By 1869, he had made four fact-finding trips to Europe.

In 1850, Gorham admitted his nephew Gorham Thurber as a partner, and another relative, Lewis Dexter, assumed a partnership position with the company in 1852. In addition to management adjustment, Gorham also realized that he could no longer rely on the traditional seven-year apprentice system to enlarge his skilled workforce, which numbered only 12 in 1850. During the 1850s, he set out to recruit more than 100 skilled craftsmen from overseas. By 1861, Gorham had increased his workforce to 150, and by the end of the Civil War, he had 312 employees. Contemporaries described him as a "practical mechanic of artistic taste, with an unusual ability to organize and construct."

In 1863, the Rhode Island legislature chartered John's firm as the Gorham Manufacturing Company, and he assumed its presidency, with Gorham Thurber designated the treasurer. Within a decade, Gorham was reputed to be the largest manufacturer of coin silverware in the world, with a workforce that had grown to 450 employees in buildings that occupied an entire block around Steeple and North Main Streets.

John Gorham had taken many financial risks in expanding his father's company, so when the Panic of 1873 hit, Gorham, like the Spragues, was forced into bankruptcy. The economic impact on John personally left him merely a Gorham Company employee when the firm recovered, so he resigned from the company in 1878. One contemporary observer noted that "he is in no business and has no means."

Sometime after 1881, John moved permanently to Chase City, Virginia, where he died on June 26, 1898. Despite this personal setback near the end of his career, his entrepreneurial spirit, inventiveness and management expertise had taken a small business founded by his father and grown it to be one of America's great industrial wonders. Although John Gorham himself had died, his creation thrived in its new and expansive complex at the end of Adelaide Avenue in the Elmwood section of Providence, to which it relocated in 1890.

Outside of his business ventures, John's personal life was relatively uneventful. In the 1840s, he attained the rank of lieutenant colonel in a militia unit called the Providence Horse Guards, and he served one year as a Whig state legislator. In 1848, he married Amey Thurber, a woman with the same name as his mother. The couple had six children, three of whom died before their father's move to Virginia. In Rhode Island, however, the Gorham name lived on through the twentieth century, and its most famous creation, the statue of the Independent Man atop Rhode Island's statehouse, crafted a year after John's death, will long be a visible reminder of the world-renowned business that Jabez and John Gorham began and nurtured.

## JOSEPH R. BROWN AND LUCIEN SHARPE

Joseph Brown and his protégé and successor Lucien Sharpe were the men who brought Rhode Island's machine tool industry into national prominence and leadership. Born a generation earlier than Lucien (1810

Joseph R. Brown.

Lucien Sharpe.

to Lucien's 1830), Joseph is more properly associated with the era covered by this book than Lucien, who lived until 1899 and performed his most notable work during America's post–Civil War Industrial Revolution, much as John Gorham did for his notable business enterprise as successor to his father, Jabez.

Joseph was born in Warren, Rhode Island, on January 26, 1810, the son of Patience Rogers of Newport and her husband, David Brown, a talented clock builder and dealer in clocks, watches, jewelry and silverware. Joseph attended school until the then-ripe age of seventeen, but he also spent considerable time in his father's shop learning and developing various mechanical skills. In 1827, after his family moved to Pawtucket, he secured a job in the machine shop of Wolcott and Harris in Valley Falls on the Blackstone River, two falls above the Wilkinson Mill. Here, Joseph engaged in the manufacture of cotton machinery and began to develop an interest in machine toolmaking.

After a brief debut in the machine-making business, he

worked with his father in the construction of tower clocks for churches in the towns of Pawtucket, Taunton and New Bedford. When Joseph became of age in 1831, he opened his own small shop and began the manufacture of tools for the clock industry, precision measuring devices, lathes and a gauge for the brass industry. Then, in 1833, his father joined him in a new venture when they acquired facilities at 60 South Main Street in Providence. From this inauspicious beginning would evolve a mammoth enterprise. In 1837, after four years of growth, this shop and its contents were destroyed by fire. With insurance proceeds of $2,000, Joseph and David moved their business across the street to 69 South Main. After 1841, Joseph became the sole proprietor when his restless father traveled west to Illinois in search of new opportunities.

As his business continued to develop, Joseph moved it to larger quarters on 115 South Main Street. At this location in 1848, he received Lucien Sharpe as an apprentice. This eighteen-year-old prospect, the son of stable owner Wilkes Sharpe and Sally Chaffee, was Providence born with family antecedents in Pomfret, Connecticut, much like Nehemiah Dodge. Sharpe, who possessed a high school education, impressed Brown not only with his mechanical aptitude but also with his drive, intelligence, literary proficiency and organizational skills. On March 1, 1853, he became Brown's partner under the firm name of J.R. Brown & Sharpe. This combination of technical and business talent thus united to make Brown & Sharpe a household name throughout Rhode Island and beyond.

When Sharpe became a partner, Brown's business had been established for twenty years, earning a local reputation for producing excellent and accurate work but earning only meager profits. Now, Brown was free to give his undivided attention to his true genius—invention—while Sharpe could focus on increasing business, most notably via an 1858 contract with the Wilcox & Gibbs Sewing Machine Company to manufacture its entire product. Giving Brown & Sharpe a prominence in mechanical work, this key account was primarily responsible for the firm's decision to focus on the precision machine tool business, in which Brown excelled.

The litany of Joseph Brown's mechanical inventions is amazing, especially to those, like historians, who generally possess little technical aptitude. Perhaps encouraged by his familiarity with clock mechanisms, Brown became interested in making precise measuring devices, the first of which was an automatic linear-dividing engine. By 1853, he had perfected the vernier caliper, the first practical tool for exact measurements that could be sold at a price affordable for the ordinary machinist. This technical breakthrough was followed by such patented inventions as a precision gear-cutting and dividing engine, a turret screw machine, the universal milling machine, the micrometer caliper, the universal grinding machine and a series of other gauges and machine tool innovations that revolutionized the industry and made Brown & Sharpe the national leader in the production of such items.

Brown was a simple, unostentatious man who was consumed by his work, which was his greatest pleasure. According to one who knew him, "He had no ambition to make a large amount of money or to establish a very large industry, but his inventions were of such a character that when made known they were at once appreciated and were of inestimable value to the business." Lucien Sharpe was the public relations and marketing genius who made them known internationally.

Brown married Caroline Niles in 1837, and the couple had two children before her death in 1851. In the following year, he married Jane Mowry of Pawtucket. As his health began to fail, he devoted more time to leisure, and the pair toured Europe in 1866 and then for an extended stay in 1867. Brown died at his summer retreat at the Isles of Shoals, New Hampshire on July 3, 1876.

During the years before and after Brown's death, Lucien Sharpe's marketing ability and managerial skill made the company one of the world's largest machine tool enterprises. In 1853, the floor space of its buildings covered 1,800 square feet; by 1899, the year of Sharpe's death, that space had increased to 293,760 square feet in seventeen interrelated buildings. During that same period, the Brown & Sharpe workforce expanded from fewer than twenty employees to two thousand craftsmen.

Sharpe avoided active involvement in politics and took no part in the management of other manufacturing or commercial enterprises, except as director (from 1874) of the Wilcox & Gibbs Sewing Machine Company. However, he was a member of the board of directors of three Providence banks and the Providence Gas Company. Most important was his position as president of the Providence Journal Company from 1886 until his death.

Lucien Sharpe married Louisa Dexter on June 25, 1857, and the couple had four daughters and two sons. His daughters married into the Chafee and Metcalf families and were prominent in the development of the Rhode Island School of Design and the funding of many local charitable agencies.

Unlike many entrepreneurs, Sharpe never retired to rest on his laurels; he was intensely focused on his business and actively managed it until the date of his death, which occurred on October 17, 1899, during his return voyage from Europe, where he had journeyed in hopes of regaining his health. He was sixty-nine years of age at his passing.

The Entrepreneurs

# WILLIAM GORHAM ANGELL

William Gorham Angell was born in Providence on November 21, 1811. He was a descendant of Thomas Angell, one of Providence's first settlers. Despite his lineage, William's family was one of modest means; his father, Enos, was a carpenter, and his mother, Catherine Gorham, one of ten children, was the sister of the soon-to-be-famous Rhode Island silversmith Jabez Gorham. Acquiring only a basic common-school education, William Angell took up his father's trade as a carpenter until he was about twenty years of age. Then he entered into a partnership with his uncle John Gorham, making reeds to allow looms to operate more efficiently. However, Angell possessed what his associates described as "an intuitive perception of the capabilities of a machine," and during these years he experimented with machinery for making iron screws to be used in woodworking.

Angell devised several improvements in the screw-making machinery of his era, and when several Providence investors formed the Eagle Screw Company in 1838 to compete with the English manufacturers of these fasteners, Angell became its agent and manager. After more than twenty successful but challenging years in business, Eagle united with the New England Company in 1860 to form the American Screw Company, with Angell as its president.

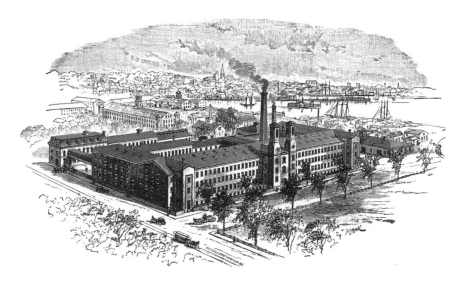

William G. Angell, founding president of the American Screw Company, presided over the construction of the New England Mill, built in 1860 at the junction of Eddy Street and Allens Avenue in South Providence. The company also operated two other large complexes in Providence: the Eagle Mill and the Bay State Mill.

Initially capitalized at $1 million, the firm soon ranked as the world's largest producer of wood and machine screws and was regarded by century's end as one of Providence's five industrial wonders of the world.

By 1860, according to one source, Angell's "long experience and mechanical skill gave him an intimate and practical acquaintance and familiarity with the entire history of the manufacture of screws and with the principle, construction, and operation of every machine used in this country or Europe for making screws." Along with his inventive ability, Angell had business sagacity and remarkable skill as an administrator. He knew intimately every aspect of his company, and he was, in addition, an excellent draftsman and a skilled architect and builder. These talents were used in the construction of factories that could stand the strain of the heavy machinery necessary in his manufacturing process. By century's end, American Screw operated three major mill complexes within the city: the Bay State Mill and the Eagle Mill, on the north and south sides of Stevens Street near Randall (now Moshassuck) Square, and the New England Mill, on Eddy Street near the junction with Allens Avenue. The company remained one of Providence's leading employers until 1949, when it moved to Willimantic, Connecticut.

Angell concentrated on his business to the exclusion of most other pursuits, but he contributed liberally, though inconspicuously, toward the relief of the poor and unfortunate. Friends commented that "he was so much engrossed with his special business that he had little or no time for anything else," be it politics, social life or amusements. It was an axiom with Angell that "a man could do but one thing well."

Angell married Ann R. Stewart in January 1836 and became the father of two sons, Edwin Gorham and William Henry. The former succeeded him as president and executive manager of the American Screw Company after William Angell's death from a lingering malady in Providence on May 13, 1870.

# George H. Corliss

Of all Rhode Island's successful entrepreneurs, manufacturers and inventors, none achieved more fame and notoriety in his lifetime than George H. Corliss, the man whose refinements to the steam engine earned him international acclaim. His ancestors were among the earliest settlers of the Massachusetts Bay Colony, where his family resided until moving to Easton, New York, a Hudson Valley village about forty miles northeast of Albany, shortly after the American Revolution. Here, George was born on June 2, 1817, to the former

Susan Sheldon and Dr. Hiram Corliss, a versatile man who farmed, taught school, ran a general store and practiced medicine.

The family, which eventually included nine children, moved to nearby Greenwich when George was eight. There he went to school and worked in the employ of a local factory store, where he inspected, measured and sold cotton goods. His first engineering venture, while he was still only seventeen, was the design of a temporary bridge over a small local river, which he constructed in ten days with volunteer help. Perhaps this feat prompted his father to support additional formal education for George, who selected Castleton Seminary in Vermont for further schooling. He graduated in 1838 but returned to Greenwich to partner with his father in operating a general store. While selling shoes at this establishment, he fielded complaints from customers that the leather shoes they purchased split along the seams. The mechanically inclined Corliss sought to address this concern by devising a stitching machine designed for work on such materials as leather and sailcloth that could sew at twenty stitches a minute. On December 23, 1843, he patented the invention and prepared to embark on a new career.

George H. Corliss.

At that time, the Providence-Pawtucket area had a national reputation for the manufacture of innovative machinery, so Corliss came to Rhode Island to find a builder for his sewing machine. He got a job as a draftsman in the shop of Fairbanks, Bancroft & Company to raise funds to produce his invention and to gain machine shop experience. Corliss's ambition and talent, coupled with the retirement of Edward Bancroft, led to the firm's reorganization in 1847, when it became Corliss, Nightingale & Company, with thirty-year-old George as its president. By 1856, it was simply the Corliss Steam Engine Company.

The upside of this business transformation was that Corliss and his company embarked on the manufacture of steam engines as the firm's principal product. The downside for Corliss was that he never put his sewing machine into production, so Elias Howe, originally of Spencer, Massachusetts, patented a slightly different version in 1846, manufactured it and received the popular acclaim for being the machine's inventor. To Howe's credit, he later acknowledged publicly, "I did not invent the sewing machine. That honor belongs to George H. Corliss of Providence, Rhode Island, the noted engine builder."

From 1847 onward, steam engine improvements and production became George's passion and his great achievement. Lacking higher education to refine his talent, Corliss sought out Alexis Caswell, a Brown professor of mathematics, to instruct him in the properties of confined steam and the force it could exert. Armed with both genius and knowledge, in 1849 Corliss patented a governor with an automatic variable cutoff, which made it possible for a steam engine to use only that amount of steam necessary to produce the required power with no loss of speed. Preventing the waste of steam by means of rationing it meant that less fuel (coal) was burned, and production costs were sharply reduced. This slide-valve mechanism operated on the same principle as Zachariah Allen's 1834 cutoff valve, but it functioned differently. The similarities eventually led to a bitter legal and highly technical verbal battle between Allen and Corliss over their respective patents, with a court ruling in favor of Corliss.

Corliss also filed numerous complaints for patent infringement against others who copied him. In total, he reputedly spent over $100,000 on such litigation, much of it paid to his principal attorney, William H. Seward of New York, who was Abraham Lincoln's secretary of state.

In his lifetime, Corliss was issued forty-eight patents, and twelve more, pending at his death, were issued later. Most involved improvements to what became known nationally as "the Corliss Engine," but others related to such diverse items as pumps, a boiler with condensing apparatus, gear cutters, machine tools and an elevator (which he installed in his mansion at 45 Prospect Street in Providence).

Immediately after creating his new firm, Corliss moved his operations from India Street to a much larger site on West River Street in Providence's north end. By the time Corliss died in 1888, the company had grown to encompass nine acres and employ one thousand people. It was the most famous engine works in America during the country's Age of Steam. Most of this vast plant has been destroyed, but the street on which Providence's mechanized main post office is located bears the Corliss name.

# The Entrepreneurs

It was at the West River Street plant that refinements were made to the Union vessel *Monitor* in 1862 to prepare it for the first battle of ironclad ships. Built at the Brooklyn Navy Yard according to the designs of Swedish inventor John Ericson, the *Monitor* had a revolving gun turret, but no factory in New York was capable of machining the large bearing on which the turret's operation depended. Corliss had such equipment, so the *Monitor*'s huge ring was rushed by train to Providence, worked on and returned to Brooklyn on the same day to make the *Monitor* ready for its epoch-making duel with the Confederate *Merrimac*.

In the ensuing years, the Corliss works produced thousands of steam engines for use throughout America and won numerous national and international awards for excellence in function and design, including coveted Rumford Medals from the American Academy of Arts and Sciences.

Corliss's crowning glory came in 1876 at the centennial celebration of the Declaration of Independence. Corliss was invited to help plan a mammoth Philadelphia exhibition of American achievements. Its centerpiece was a 776-ton Corliss engine that was 40 feet high with a flywheel 30 feet in diameter and weighing 11 tons. The wheel meshed with a pinion shaft that was 325 feet long and delivered power to the hundreds of machines that were on display in the exhibition's thirteen-acre main hall. The Centennial Engine, as it was called, was built in Providence and shipped by train on seventy-one flat cars to Philadelphia. Corliss, a devout Congregationalist, refused to place his engine in service on the scheduled Sabbath Day, so on Wednesday, May 10, 1876, as the spectators stood in awe, George, his wife Emily, President Ulysses Grant and Brazilian emperor Dom Pedro II presided over the start-up ceremony, making the great wheel revolve to set in motion the intricate mechanisms that powered eight thousand machines throughout the vast hall.

Corliss spent $100,000 on his prize creation, which ran flawlessly during the six-month festival. The engine was then bought for $62,000 by George Pullman, of railroad car fame, for his company town in Illinois. In 1905, as electricity replaced steam power, the famed machine was sold for scrap at a price of $7,892.50.

George Corliss did not have far-ranging interests other than his work, except for his skill as an architect. He dabbled a little in politics, serving in the Rhode Island General Assembly from 1868 to 1870. He also was a Republican elector in the highly disputed Rutherford Hayes–Samuel Tilden presidential contest of 1876, decided in favor of Republican Hayes by one electoral vote. Corliss was married twice, first in 1839 to Phoebe Frost, who died in 1859 after providing him with a son and a daughter, and then in 1866 to Emily Shaw, from his ancestral hometown of Newburyport.

For his second wife, who was considerably younger, Corliss built a splendidly designed mansion at 45 Prospect Street with a stunning interior, an advanced radiant heating system with thermostats and a hydraulic elevator from the basement to the third floor. He died in this mansion (which he called Emily's "Bermuda home") on February 21, 1888. Emily long survived him, living until 1910, but her husband's business did not; it failed in the disastrous national economic panic of 1893.

# ZACHARIAH ALLEN

Zachariah Allen was a man with a distinguished Rhode Island lineage and a record of personal achievement that was even more distinguished. He was born in Providence on September 15, 1795, the son of Anne Crawford and Zachariah Allen, a talented and innovative calico printer. His older brother Philip would also become a calico printer, as well as governor of Rhode Island and a United States senator; his older sister Lydia became

Zachariah Allen.

the mother of Governor Thomas Wilson Dorr. As a son of well-to-do parents, Zachariah was educated at a private school in Medford, Massachusetts, at Phillips Exeter Academy and at Brown University, from which he graduated in 1813.

Very shortly after leaving Brown, Zachariah was actively involved in business and municipal affairs. He studied law under James Burrill Jr. (whose profile will follow) and passed the bar in 1815, but law did not suit his scientific mind, so he studied medicine briefly at the Brown Medical School, receiving a certificate of proficiency but not a degree. Having turned away from the practice of law and medicine, he began a remarkable career as a scientist, inventor, businessman, author, civil servant and reformer.

Allen had a flair for hydraulics and civil engineering and studied the latter in Europe in 1825 as a prelude to publishing his first book, entitled *The Science of Mechanics Applied to the Useful Arts in Europe and America*. The application of water to firefighting and to manufacturing engaged his attention in the 1820s. He introduced Providence's original hydraulion (i.e., suction fire engine and hose equipment) in 1822 to replace the hand buckets then in use, and as a member of the town council from 1820 to 1823, he became the principal advocate for the establishment of the Providence waterworks system.

His interest in firefighting went beyond the mere technical; a volunteer fireman himself, in 1829 Allen was a founder and trustee of the Providence Association of Firemen for Mutual Assistance, which provided help to the families of firemen injured or killed in the line of duty. In 1835, he combined fire protection with his business endeavors. Upset by the cost of conventional insurance for his Allendale woolen mill (which he established in North Providence in 1822 and built with a great attention to fire safety), Allen founded a mutual fire insurance company devoted exclusively to insuring factories against fire loss. This business, originally called the Manufacturers' Mutual Fire Insurance Company (now FM Global of Johnston), was the pioneer in the famous Factory Mutual System. It was Allen who first developed a procedure for inspecting and rating factory buildings and setting their premiums based on their condition, their method of construction and the quality of the fire prevention apparatus they installed. His formula drastically lowered fire insurance rates for those businesses that practiced fire safety. As one historian of the insurance industry has stated, "Allen took the first step toward adapting the mutual idea to meet the needs of the business community and began the integration of mutual insurance into the commercial life of the nation."

Zachariah's Allendale Mill, which sparked his insurance idea, was also the beneficiary of his genius. Built in 1822 on the Woonasquatucket River from the designs of architect John Holden Greene, the mill's charter contained the first systematic plans for constructing reservoirs for such hydraulic purposes as "retaining flood waters for use during the droughts of summer." At this facility, Allen devised and patented a rolling process to impart a gloss finish to cloth and pioneered the use of a power loom for the manufacture of broadcloth.

Among Allen's many other industrial patents were a central furnace system for heating by hot air, a cloth napping machine, a device for spooling wool, the automatic steam engine cutoff valve (which later became the subject of an acrimonious patent infringement debate with George Corliss) and a method of transmitting power by leather belting in place of the gear or "cogwheel" connections previously employed. This transmission of power fascinated Allen. It inspired his 1851 treatise entitled *The Philosophy of the Mechanics of Nature, and of the Source and Modes of Transmission of Natural Motive Power* and his later address to the New England Cotton Manufacturers' Association on the "Best Modes of Transmission of Power from Motors to Machines." In the early 1840s, this fascination took him to Niagara Falls, where Allen made the earliest measurement of the volume of water and the extent of water power over the 160-foot-high cataract. His account, published in the April 1844 issue of Stillman's *Scientific Journal*, concluded that the effective force of this water was over seven million horsepower.

Allen remained active in the textile industry until 1871, despite a loss of ownership due to bankruptcy caused by the national economic panic of 1857. In addition to the Allendale Mill (as its owner-manager from 1822 to 1857), he had ownership interests in the Phenix Mill (West Warwick) from 1835 to 1854 and the Georgiaville Mill (Smithfield). He also served as manager of his brother Philip's Allen Printworks from 1857 to 1871. He managed these facilities in a paternalistic, hands-on manner, demonstrating great solicitude for the welfare of his workers by paying them good wages and furnishing them with educational and religious amenities.

But business, science and internationally acclaimed scientific writings (of which there were several) did not exhaust the talents or interests of Allen. He loved books, especially histories; he lectured widely on local historical topics; he sponsored a pioneering free evening school for Providence workers in 1840; he helped to establish the Providence Athenaeum in 1831 and the Providence Public Library in 1878; he served as a trustee of Brown University for over fifty years; he was active in the development of Roger Williams Park and its museum of natural history in the early 1870s; and he held the presidency of the Rhode Island Historical Society for many years.

When in England in 1825, he commissioned a handwritten copy of Roger Williams's famous Native American ethnology *A Key into the Language of America* from the Bodleian Library at Oxford University. This work was first published by Gregory Dexter of Providence in 1643. Allen gave this transcript to the Rhode Island Historical Society, and it was eventually republished as the first volume of the society's historical collections. Throughout his life, he championed the rights of Native Americans, earning him letters of thanks from as far distant as the Ojibway and Potawatomie tribes. He was instrumental in the erection of monuments to Chief Sachem Massasoit and his son, King Philip, both of whom have joined Allen in the Rhode Island Heritage Hall of Fame.

Other recipients of Allen's support and philanthropy were Butler Hospital for the mentally ill, where he directed and helped finance the construction of its original buildings; his alma mater, Brown University; the Rhode Island state prison, the Providence waterworks (his earliest successful project); and the Rhode Island Historical Society, where his voluminous papers have been deposited.

In 1817, Allen married Eliza Harriet Arnold, the daughter of wealthy Providence merchant Welcome Arnold. The couple had three daughters. They resided in a modest home at 1093 Smith Street, which was added to the National Register of Historic Places in 1994. Active to the end, the widowed Allen died in Providence at the age of eighty-six on March 17, 1882.

## ROWLAND GIBSON HAZARD

Rowland Gibson Hazard was born in South Kingstown, Rhode Island, on October 9, 1801, the fourth of nine children of Rowland Hazard and Mary Peace of Charleston, South Carolina, where his father had established trading contacts. In 1819, with his brother Isaac, Rowland assumed control of his father's small woolen mill in Peace Dale, a South Kingstown village his father had named for his mother's family. He had primary responsibility for marketing products to southern plantation owners in Louisiana, Alabama and Mississippi, and he wintered in New Orleans from about 1833 to 1842. His experience in the South and his Quaker faith led him to develop a hatred for slavery and to work on behalf of kidnapped free blacks in Louisiana. He secured the liberation of several unfortunate captives, a feat he regarded as the greatest of his many accomplishments.

Rowland Gibson Hazard.

The family's woolen mill partnership, incorporated as the Peace Dale Manufacturing Company in 1848, became one of the largest businesses in the southern part of the state. Hazard eventually expanded his operations to another mill in neighboring Charlestown and gave its village the name Carolina, in honor of his wife.

Hazard also authored eleven books and a wide variety of articles, mostly on philosophical subjects, which gained for him an intimate intellectual relationship with the Reverend William Ellery Channing. His 1841 essay, "Causes of Decline of Political Morality," influenced the ban on lotteries in Rhode Island's 1843 constitution. In 1849, he became a leading advocate of the regulation of railroad trusts, and his treatise on "The Relations of Railroad Corporation to the Public" led to a series of tumultuous state legislative hearings. He served intermittently in the state legislature—as a South Kingstown representative in 1851–52, 1854–55 and 1880–81 and as a senator in 1866–67. Hazard was a Rhode Island delegate to the founding conventions of the Republican Party at Pittsburgh and Philadelphia in 1856, drafted the economic planks for the national Republican campaign platforms in 1860 and 1868 and played an important role in planning the Union economy during the Civil War.

Hazard did much to sustain our national credit at home and abroad, especially when the Union cause looked bleak. His newspaper articles on public finance were collected and published in pamphlet form, mainly by bankers in New York for foreign readers. These essays induced European bankers to overcome their skepticism about the war's outcome and hold or increase their investments in United States war bonds. In this endeavor, Hazard worked in concert with President Lincoln and Treasury Secretary Salmon P. Chase, the father of Kate Chase Sprague, who was the wife of William Sprague III, Rhode Island's Civil War governor.

In 1866, Hazard retired from the textile business and invested heavily in the Union Pacific Railroad, with the understanding that his involvement would be purely financial and would not interfere with his retirement. After the company fell into financial disarray and became embroiled in the Credit Mobilier scandal, Hazard spent much of his final years setting its affairs straight. He was one of the few investors to emerge from that railroad construction fiasco with his reputation unscathed.

As a philanthropist and humanitarian, Hazard was a prominent supporter of Butler Hospital in Providence and a trustee and fellow of Brown University, where he endowed a chair of physics with a $40,000 gift. To his native South Kingstown, particularly his home village of Peace Dale, Hazard donated money for schools, churches, the town hall, the library and other civic improvements. He also provided steady financial support to Rhode Island's abolition, temperance, free religion and women's suffrage movements, and he frequently interacted with female reformers such as Paulina Wright Davis and Elizabeth Buffum Chace to advance these causes.

Rowland Gibson Hazard was significant on the national and international scene for both his financial activities and his writings on philosophical subjects. He corresponded often with its influential British economist John Stuart Mill, who expressed admiration for Hazard's theoretical treatises. In a letter to Hazard, Mill wrote: "I wish you had nothing to do but philosophize; for though I do not often agree with you, I see in everything you write a well-marked natural capacity for philosophy."

In 1828, Hazard married Caroline Newbold (1807–1868) of Bloomsdale, Pennsylvania. They had two sons who continued the operation of the South County woolen mills and their father's other holdings after Rowland's retirement from the business. The younger son was John Newbold Hazard (1836–1900); the elder, Rowland Hazard II (1829–1898), came to equal his remarkable father as a philanthropist, industrialist and businessman (including his own acquisition of large mining interests in Missouri). His daughter, Caroline Hazard, became a noted author and educator and the benefactor and longtime president of Wellesley College. Rowland II is so designated, not to distinguish him from his versatile father, who had the middle name "Gibson," but in deference to his grandfather, who pioneered woolen manufacturing in South Kingstown.

After a long life embracing such diverse fields as business, economics, mathematics, politics, philanthropy, philosophy and a variety of reform causes, Rowland Gibson Hazard died peacefully at Peace Dale on June 24, 1888, in his eighty-seventh year. Few Rhode Islanders, if any, matched him in the range of his talents and interests.

A large collection of the Hazard family papers is maintained at the library of the Rhode Island Historical Society, and the Harvard University Business School possesses a quantity of Peace Dale Manufacturing Company records. Rowland Gibson Hazard's granddaughter, Caroline, edited and published a four-volume edition of his writings in 1889.

# II

# THE PHILANTHROPISTS

## NICHOLAS BROWN II

Nicholas Brown II (the Roman numeral is used here to distinguish him from his noteworthy father) was born in Providence in 1769, one of the ten children of Rhoda Jenkes Brown, who died when young Nicholas was only fourteen. In 1786, he graduated from Rhode Island College (now a university that bears his surname) and went to work in his father's counting house. Then, in 1792, a year after the sudden death of his father, he joined his father's mercantile firm of Brown & Benson. Four years later, after the retirement of George Benson, he became a partner with Thomas Pointon Ives in this commercial company, which then assumed the name of Brown & Ives, under which part of the family interests are still managed. The merger became familial when Ives married Hope Brown, Nicholas's sister.

Nicholas was blessed with much more than a powerful and wealthy father; he also had three distinguished and influential uncles—merchant, scientist and architect Joseph Brown, reformer and entrepreneur Moses Brown and merchant and political leader John Brown, Providence's most prominent citizen. Nicholas's life, as the only surviving son of a wealthy father, would become a cardinal illustration of the maxim "Of him to whom much has been given, much is expected."

The first ventures of Brown & Ives were mercantile in nature, building on the initiatives of John Brown, who had opened a trade between Providence and the Orient in 1787. One of the most famous East Indiamen was the Brown & Ives vessel *Ann and Hope*, named for the owners' wives. The firm also applied that name to its Lonsdale textile mill after the 550-ton ship sank

Nicholas Brown II.

off Block Island in January 1806 during a wintry storm. For the half century that it lasted, the China trade brought wealth to Nicholas and his main rival, Edward Carrington, and this exotic commerce became a source of work and wonder for many Providence mariners. The company sold the *Hanover*, its last East Indiaman, in 1838.

Nicholas not only followed his uncle John's lead in trade, but he also followed the lead of his uncle Moses in the emerging business of manufacturing. In 1804, Brown & Ives bought its first water rights on the power-producing Blackstone River to begin the production of cotton textiles. By 1834, when it created the huge Lonsdale Company, Brown & Ives ranked among the major textile manufacturers in America. The more mechanically inclined Thomas Ives ran the operations of the various mills until his death in 1835, while Nicholas handled the marketing side of the partners' numerous businesses.

Nicholas achieved wealth through his commercial and industrial dealings, but he achieved lasting fame and influence through his philanthropic endeavors. In 1770, his uncles had brought Rhode Island College, a Baptist institution, to Providence from its 1764 birthplace in Warren; however, it was Nicholas who became the school's principal benefactor, prompting it to adopt his surname.

Nicholas became a trustee of the college in 1791 and its treasurer from 1796 until 1825. In 1804, he gave it his first of many gifts—law books and $5,000 for the endowment of a professorship of oratory and belles-lettres. The college responded by changing its name to Brown. In 1823, he and his nephew funded Hope College on the Brown campus, named after his sister Hope (Brown) Ives and his grandmother Hope (Power) Brown. In 1834, he furnished the funds for Manning Hall, built in honor of the Reverend James Manning, the institution's first president. Just prior to his death, he gave $10,000 toward the construction of Rhode Island Hall and the president's house. Other gifts of books, land and money brought his total benefactions to the college to approximately $160,000, an enormous sum for those times.

But the generosity of Nicholas extended far beyond the campus of his alma mater. He helped to found the Providence Athenaeum, funded Baptist literary and missionary causes and left $30,000 in his will for the care of the insane that assisted in the establishment of Butler Hospital in Providence. There was some irony in this gift: in an 1835 letter, his rebellious and ungrateful son, Nicholas III, called his father "a lunatic" for giving so much money to charity.

Brown's president, the Reverend Francis Wayland, who was recruited by Nicholas, said of him that he had a large heart full of "active sympathy for every form of human suffering. He not infrequently visited the sick in their own dwellings, while his door was frequently thronged, and his steps waylaid by poor and unfortunate of every age."

Here it is worthy of note that the cousin of Nicholas and his business associate, Obadiah Brown (the son of Moses Brown), rivaled Nicholas in generosity. Obadiah's profits from a partnership that included his father Moses, William Almy, Samuel Slater and Slater's brother John were directed in large measure to the Quaker Yearly Meeting School (now named Moses Brown) in Providence, which he supported during his lifetime and to which he left a bequest of $100,000 upon his death in 1822.

Nicholas Brown's financial strength brought him political influence. He served Providence in the General Assembly from 1807 to 1821, both as a senator and a representative. He was a staunch Federalist who opposed the War of 1812 because of its detrimental impact on commerce, and he held strongly to Federalist principles, especially the responsibility of the aristocracy of wealth and intelligence to run the government and lead society. Despite his concern for the less fortunate, he was wary of their influence on politics. Nicholas had a conservative temperament that looked with disdain on populist movements and reform protests by unruly agitators. He prized order and stability. After the demise of the Federalist Party, he became a Whig and served as an elector for William Henry Harrison in 1840.

Nicholas married well in 1791, when he chose the daughter of John Carter, Providence's postmaster and its foremost journalist, as his bride. Unfortunately, Ann Carter died seven years later. Among their four children were Ann, who married future Democratic governor John Brown Francis, and John Carter Brown, the bibliophile and benefactor of Brown University. Nicholas took Mary Bowen Stelle as his second wife in 1801, but she died in 1836 without issue. He succumbed after a long illness on September 27, 1841, at the age of seventy-two.

# EBENEZER KNIGHT DEXTER

Ebenezer Knight Dexter, the man who became Providence's greatest benefactor, was born in Providence on April 26, 1773, to Phebe (Harris) Dexter, the second wife of Colonel Knight Dexter. Both parents were descendants of Providence's earliest settlers. Ebenezer's lineage gave him political and financial connections that he used to good advantage as a merchant and real estate speculator and developer.

The details of Dexter's business ventures are obscure, other than the assertion by a contemporary that "he pursued his business with such strict attention that he was able to retire with a fortune [at a time] when most men think of accumulating one," but the use to which Dexter put his money is highly visible in Providence to this day.

His association with Governor James Fenner, David Howell (a Brown University professor of law and a U.S. District Court judge) and David's son Jeremiah Brown Howell (Rhode Island's Democratic-Republican senator) led to his appointment as U.S. marshal for Rhode Island, a post more prestigious than profitable and one productive of controversy before and during the War of 1812. The party of Jefferson and Madison had enacted a series of commercial restrictions (including an embargo on all seaborne commerce and several nonintercourse acts) in an attempt to use economic coercion to force the warring powers of England and France to respect America's rights on the high seas. The Federalist Party, strong in

Ebenezer Knight Dexter.

Providence, and the merchant houses of Edward Carrington and Nicholas Brown vigorously opposed these trade-stifling measures. As U.S. marshal, Dexter was sworn to enforce them. Judge William R. Staples, in his 1843 *Annals of the Town of Providence*, comments on Dexter's dilemma:

> *He held the office in a most inauspicious time for himself. During the embargo, non-intercourse and war, his duties were arduous, and sometimes directly contravening the wishes and the interests of a large portion of this community. Yet, he so carefully and skillfully managed, that he lost not the esteem and respect of his fellow townsmen, nor the confidence of the government.*

Dexter was not only perplexed by political problems, but he also suffered personal losses. His wife of eighteen years, Waitstill Howell, daughter of Mary Brown and David Howell, died in May 1819, a few weeks prior to her forty-third birthday. Their only child, Mary, died in infancy, leaving Ebenezer with no direct heirs and Providence his beneficiary.

The midsummer of 1824 was a noteworthy time in Providence. On July 21, Dexter's father-in-law, Judge David Howell, died. Three weeks later, on

August 10, Dexter himself passed away after a long illness. No sooner was Dexter interred in the North Burial Ground than the Marquis de Lafayette returned to Providence on August 23 as part of his whirlwind American tour. Here he was greeted and feted by the town's adoring citizenry.

The public reading of Dexter's last will and testament did not generate the excitement of Lafayette's visit, but it generated an appreciation that has lasted much longer. On November 22, 1824, the town meeting accepted Dexter's bequest, which included gifts of two large parcels of land—one on the East Side, consisting of nearly forty acres, and another in the West End, comprising nearly ten acres—plus some smaller parcels, bringing the land donation to more than fifty-two acres. The resolution of acceptance read, in part, as follows:

> *Whereas, the late Ebenezer Knight Dexter, Esq., our lamented fellow citizen, actuated by a spirit of munificence and benevolence, worthy of all praise and honorable to the community of which he was a member, did in and by his last will and testament, after providing for individual objects of his attachment, constitute this his native town [as] his residuary devisee and legatee of estates real and personal wherewith it pleased Divine Providence to bless him, in this life, by means of which most liberal donation a very large and efficient fund, under the conditions of said will remains at the disposal and control of the town, for effecting the judicious intentions of said deceased, and especially ameliorating the condition of the unfortunate poor, for whose comfortable support and permanent and creditable relief, it appears to be the principal object of the testator in his bounty to provide... an act...of such tender concern for the cause of suffering humanity ought to be met by the most open and sincere acknowledgment and acceptance.*

The largest tract, located off Hope Street near Moses Brown School, was given for use as a poor farm. A huge almshouse for paupers, called Dexter Asylum, was opened there in 1828 and completed in 1830 from the designs of architect John Holden Greene. The asylum, endowed by funds from Dexter's bequest, was altered and enlarged in 1870, and its architectural style changed from classical Roman-Doric to French Empire. In accordance with Dexter's wishes, the estate on which the building stood was enclosed by a long stone wall 3 feet wide at the base, 8 feet high and 6,220 feet in length.

The property was purchased from the city by Brown University in 1957 for $1,000,777, a sum that was earmarked by the city for poor relief as the Ebenezer Knight Dexter Trust Fund. Brown subsequently erected its

George V. Meehan Auditorium and a modern athletic complex on the asylum grounds. The Dexter Asylum building was demolished in 1958, but most of the wall survives.

Another tract in this great philanthropist's donation is the Dexter Training Grounds, a ten-acre parcel on which the Cranston Street Armory was constructed in 1907–8. This land was designated by its grantor as a site for the training of militia. Both the land and the financial proceeds from Dexter's bequest are managed by the Commissioners of the Dexter Donation, a permanent five-man agency chaired by the mayor of Providence, allowing Dexter's benign influence to live on into the twenty-first century.

Fittingly, Dexter's presence is still in evidence on his training grounds, primarily through the efforts of Henry C. Clark, then the president of the Providence Coal Company. In 1893, as a result of Clark's donation, local sculptor Hippolyte L. Hubert crafted an eight-foot-high bronze statue of Dexter for the site. On its nine-foot-high pedestal is inscribed an eloquent testimony to individuals such as Ebenezer Knight Dexter: "Leaving nothing but a headstone to mark our passage through life does not make the world better. They live best who serve humanity the most."

# EDWARD HARRIS

Edward Harris was northern Rhode Island's major manufacturer, an ardent abolitionist, a generous philanthropist, one of the principal founders of the state's Republican Party and the leading citizen of mid-nineteenth-century Woonsocket.

Harris was born on October 3, 1801, in the village of Limerock (now in the town of Lincoln), the son of David F. and Lydia (Streeter) Harris. His Quaker parents moved to Dutchess County, New York, when Edward was a child and then journeyed farther westward to Ashtabula, Ohio, on the shore of Lake Erie. Little is known of Edward's childhood experiences or education, but as a young man he farmed and had enough basic learning to teach school.

In 1823, Harris returned to northern Rhode Island and became an assistant in the Valley Falls counting house of his uncle William Harris, a successful textile manufacturer. In the following year, he moved northward on the Blackstone River to Albion, where his uncles William and Samuel Harris also owned a mill in partnership with Abraham and Isaac Wilkinson. Within two years, Edward Harris earned a promotion to the position of factory superintendent, but he left that job in November 1828 to become the agent of the Harris Lime Rock Company in the village where he was born twenty-seven years before.

With capital from savings of $2,500 and $1,000 more from his father, he left his family's employ in March 1831 to open a mill for the production of satinet on the falls of the Blackstone River in present-day Woonsocket. At first, he had two partners, but by 1837, he had built Mill No. 2 and had become a sole proprietor. This second mill produced merino cassimere. In 1844,

Edward Harris.

Harris built Mill No. 3, a large brick and stone structure in the central part of Woonsocket, near Market Square. This plant was followed a year later by Mill No. 4, the only one of his factories still standing. All of these mills were run by water power from Woonsocket Falls, supplemented by steam power, and later became known as the "old mills." By the mid-1850s, they contained twenty-five sets of wool cards and turned out twelve thousand yards of the best "Harris Cassimeres" every week.

Edward Harris's Mill No. 5, built in the 1850s, specialized in cotton production on its seven thousand spindles. In 1860, Harris commenced construction of Mill No. 6, the Privilege Mill complex, his greatest industrial creation. Upon completion five years later, this L-shaped structure on the Mill River, a Blackstone tributary, measured 442 feet in length by 60 feet in width and rose five stories high. It contained a 175-horsepower Corliss engine and a 40-foot-high waterwheel with a 28-foot breast. Connected to this mammoth building were a dye house, a picker house, a foundry, a planning and sawmill, a horseshoe-shaped dam that created Harris Pond and eighty houses containing 250 tenements for the factory's workforce. To sell the huge quantity of woolen and cotton goods produced in these establishments, Harris opened a warehouse in New York City in 1855 and retained an exclusive agent there to market his nationally known Harris Cassimeres.

According to a contemporary observer, Harris had a "robust constitution, clear head, and great energy," qualities essential for his hands-on management of such a huge enterprise. "Rising early, he attended to the details of his extensive business, and would not trust to others what he could do himself." To his manufacturing endeavors, Harris added the presidency of two area banks.

The great wealth that Harris accumulated in the operation of his six mills brought great influence and the ability to share his fortune. Edward Harris's generosity became legendary. True to his Quaker roots, he vigorously supported the abolitionist movement and donated to that cause. In 1859, when John Brown was in prison under sentence of death for his bold raid on the federal arsenal at Harpers Ferry, Virginia, to get arms for a slave uprising, Harris sent him a consoling letter with a $100 check for Brown's bereft family. When his marketing agent advised Harris to remove his name from his fabrics so as not to incur a Southern boycott, he defiantly put his label on both ends of each piece of his cassimeres. In addition to his antislavery efforts, Harris vigorously supported the temperance movement of the 1850s and its political candidates.

Harris himself was no stranger to politics. By mid-life, he had served in each house of the General Assembly, and he ran as the Free-Soil candidate for Rhode Island governor in 1849, 1850, 1851 and 1853. As the standard-bearer for this controversial third party, he never polled more than the 783 votes he garnered in 1850.

After the passage by a Democratic Congress of the Kansas-Nebraska Act of 1854, opening the U.S. territories to the possibility of slavery, Harris joined a movement to create a political party whose basic tenet was opposition to the extension of slavery to the territories, a position originally held by the Free-Soil Party. As a founder of that new faction in Rhode Island, he joined reformer Rowland Hazard and other locals in 1856 at the organizational meeting of the national Republican Party in Pittsburgh and then attended the first Republican convention in Philadelphia, a gathering that nominated the western pathfinder John C. Fremont for president. Four years later, the next Republican presidential candidate, Abraham Lincoln, came to Woonsocket on March 8, 1860, at the invitation of Harris to deliver a major address at a large meeting hall that Harris had built in 1856. When the votes were counted in Rhode Island, Lincoln easily defeated Democrat Stephen Douglas in the state's presidential contest of 1860.

That 1856 structure on Main Street, called the Harris Institute, is now part of the Woonsocket City Hall. It was donated by Harris to his fellow townsmen in 1863 as a facility "for the purpose of promoting the moral, intellectual, and social improvement of the inhabitants of the district." The Harris Institute contained a free public library, a large third-floor lecture hall (where Lincoln had spoken), three stores and a post office. (The use of the words "inhabitants of the district" in the Harris grant needs explanation. Although one speaks of Harris's donations as having been made to Woonsocket, that political entity did not in fact exist until January 31, 1867, when the mill villages of Woonsocket Falls, Social, Clinton and Jenckesville on the north and east side of the Blackstone were set off from Cumberland and incorporated as a new town. On March 8, 1871, the south and west bank villages of Hamlet, Bernon and Globe were taken from Smithfield to round out the present municipality.)

The Harris Institute was only one of the many gifts bestowed on Woonsocket by the philanthropy of Edward Harris. He also constructed new streets, provided a public water system and donated sites for the town's high school, a district school and the Oak Hill Cemetery. Contemporaries have estimated that the total of his local benefactions was around $500,000 in the currency of his day.

Harris's benevolence was not merely confined to Woonsocket or to such national reform causes as abolitionism and temperance. In 1847, during the Irish famine, Harris donated the sum of $500 for relief, and his brother-in-law Welcome Farnum, also a textile magnate, gave $1,000. These were the largest individual contributions to that cause recorded in Rhode Island and among the highest in the nation.

In December 1835, Harris married Rachel Farnum of Blackstone, Massachusetts, who died in 1846, leaving a son and a daughter. Harris then married his second wife, Abby Metcalf of Cumberland, who gave him four more children and survived him. Harris died on November 24, 1872, at Oakley, his Woonsocket home at the corner of Blackstone Street and Harris Avenue, where Lincoln had stayed. Harris is buried with his family in the Oak Hill Cemetery.

It would not be an exaggeration to state that the donations of Edward Harris to his town far exceeded gifts for a similar purpose made by any other Rhode Islander, ever.

## John Carter Brown

John Carter Brown is yet another member of the distinguished and ubiquitous Brown family of Providence Plantations—begun by Chad Brown in 1638—to secure election to the Rhode Island Heritage Hall of Fame. In August 1797, John became the youngest of the four children born to Nicholas Brown II and Ann Carter, the daughter of printer John Carter

John Carter Brown.

(profiled in *Rhode Island's Founders*). His mother died less than a year after his birth.

John received his AB degree from Brown (where else?) in 1816 and was immediately impressed by his father into the firm of Brown & Ives. Soon after, he was dispatched to Ohio (where Rhode Island land speculators had ventured as early as the 1780s) and westward to inspect tracts for purchase. Somewhat bookish and genteel, he found this task unappealing, but being of a generous nature, he later made monetary gifts to several societies and institutions in this developing area. John's tastes were for cultured travel and the amenities of life rather than for the chores and demands of business, but for his father's sake he accepted his obligations to Brown & Ives and became a partner in 1832. His older brother, Nicholas III, defiantly left Rhode Island for extensive and extended travel in Europe, causing his father great disappointment.

John himself had the means and found the time to travel, to pursue historical studies and to collect books—his first love. He resided in Europe from 1823 to 1826 and bought many rare volumes there, which he donated to Brown upon his return. In gratitude, the college made him a trustee in 1828 and a fellow in 1842 after the death of his father.

At first, his collecting lacked focus. He initially sought classic books with fine bindings, illustrated volumes, letterpress books, rare polyglot Bibles and sets by noted authors—what experts call "a gentleman's library." But among his first purchases were several of the earliest accounts of New England's settlement in which he made margined notes of all references to Rhode Island.

Gradually, John began to concentrate his efforts on the acquisition of books relating to the discovery and early settlement of the New World. He used as guides White Kennet's *Bibliothecae Americane Primordia* (1713);

# The Philanthropists

*Bibliothèque Americaine*, compiled by Henri-Terrnaux-Compan (1837); and the catalogues of Obadiah Rich. Between 1841 and 1847, he acquired his father's library (which he purchased from his brother Nicholas III) and over fifteen hundred volumes of Americana from Henry Stevens, a New England book dealer who had moved to London. During the ensuing years, John purchased regularly from Stevens's catalogues. By the 1860s, his collection, which Brown called Bibliotheca Americana, overflowed his house, requiring a fireproof addition. At this point, Rhode Island's secretary of state John Russell Bartlett prepared a printed catalogue of his acquisitions, which he continued to revise and update until 1882. Ironically, some of Brown's books had been acquired from Bartlett when the secretary of state operated a New York City bookstore during the 1840s.

Continuing his father's tradition of *noblesse oblige*, John made numerous donations to Brown during his lifetime. His gifts in the form of books, land and buildings, including a new university library, equaled those of his father. In emulation of Nicholas II, John also made substantial donations to Butler Hospital and, when Rhode Island Hospital opened in 1867, to that institution as well.

John's earlier business contacts in the Midwest and his hostility to slavery prompted him to play a prominent role in the Free-Soil Movement of the 1840s and '50s. He joined the New England Emigrant Aid Society and became its president in 1854, the year Congress passed Stephen Douglas's controversial Kansas-Nebraska Act, thereby opening all U.S. territories to the possibility of slavery extension via the doctrine of popular sovereignty. This company sent more than two thousand antislavery settlers into Kansas, a noble effort but one that helped to precipitate an armed conflict with slaveholders for control of that territory's government, known infamously as "Bleeding Kansas," a major milestone on the road to the Civil War.

On June 10, 1874, John Carter Brown died, leaving a widow, Sophia Augusta Brown (no blood relation), the daughter of Patrick Brown, an associate justice of the General Court of the Bahama Islands. The couple, who married in 1859, had three children. At the time of John's death, his special collection had grown to 7,500 volumes. In 1898, Sophia transferred title to this constantly expanding treasure-trove of Americana to her eldest son, John Nicholas. When he died in 1900, John Nicholas Brown's will provided that the library, which he had further enlarged, be deeded to Brown University with an endowment fund of $500,000 for future accessions, plus a $150,000 gift to erect a special building to house it. That structure, the John Carter Brown Library, opened on May 17, 1904, thirty years after the bibliophile's death.

# III

# THE MULTIFACETED POLITICIANS

## U.S. SENATOR, CHIEF JUSTICE AND SPEAKER JAMES BURRILL JR.

James Burrill Jr., a brilliant leader of the early nineteenth-century Rhode Island bar and a noted orator, was born in Providence on April 25, 1772, the son of James and Elizabeth (Rawson) Burrill. He received his early education in the private school of William Wilkinson and then entered Brown, graduating in the class of 1788 at the age of sixteen. After legal clerkships, first in the office of U.S. senator Theodore Foster and then under the tutelage of Judge David Howell, he became state's attorney general in 1797 at the age of twenty-five and served in that annually elected post until 1813, when he was chosen a member of the Rhode Island House of Representatives. Within a year, he was elevated to the position of Speaker, then the most powerful position in Rhode Island's government. In 1816, he was made chief justice of the state's Supreme Court for a year when such appointments were made by the General Assembly on an annual basis.

In 1806, when the northern half of Glocester was set off as a separate town, it was named in Burrill's honor, even though, at age thirty-four, he had not yet reached the pinnacle of his remarkable political career.

Burrill's lone reversal during this long run of political successes came in November 1810, when he lost the General Assembly vote for U.S. senator to Democratic-Republican Jeremiah Brown Howell by a margin of forty-two to forty-one. Under the charter regime the governor could vote as a member of the Grand Committee (the House and Senate sitting jointly). The legislative journal for this contest reads, "His Excellency the Governor

[Democratic-Republican James Fenner] having voted in the first instance as one of the committee and not having the vote as presiding officer."

Shortly after assuming the chief justiceship, Burrill avenged his 1810 defeat when he was elected by the legislature to the United States Senate as a Federalist. He began his term in December 1817 as the successor to Howell, but he died in office on Christmas Day 1820 after serving only half his term. During his short tenure in Congress, he became chairman of the Senate's Judiciary

U.S. senator, chief justice and Speaker James Burrill Jr.

Committee. His last major speech on December 7, 1820, was in unsuccessful opposition to a provision of the Missouri Compromise, a major piece of legislation that provided for Maine to be set off from Massachusetts and admitted as a free state, balanced by the admission of Missouri as a slave state. The bill contained a provision that banned free blacks and mulattos from settling in Missouri. This clause, said Burrill, "was entirely repugnant to the Constitution of the United States" because it distinguished between classes of citizens.

Senator Burrill's older brother, George R. Burrill, who was also a distinguished lawyer and orator, is regarded as Rhode Island's first notable constitutional reformer. In 1807, George wrote a controversial, path-breaking pamphlet that he published anonymously as *A Few Observations on the Government of the State of Rhode Island*. This treatise by the Providence Federalist was the first extensive attack on the continued adequacy of the Charter of 1663 as Rhode Island's basic law. George Burrill, the presumed author, questioned the very validity of the Royal Charter because it had failed to receive the ratification of a popular convention after America's independence was declared. He then voiced criticism of the charter's apportionment of the General Assembly and lamented the document's failure to conform to the recently espoused theory of separated powers.

George, himself a legislator, also complained of the omnipotence of the General Assembly and the dominance of that body over the governor and the judiciary. Finally, he alleged that the government as presently organized failed to provide properly for either education or the militia. The proposed remedy for these deplorable conditions, he urged, was a written constitution, framed by a convention and ratified by the people, with the uncooperative General Assembly bypassed in the process. It is not known whether his brother James supported these bold assertions.

On the personal side, James Burrill married Sally Arnold in 1797 and fathered four daughters, two of whom provided him with very distinguished descendants. Burrill was the great-grandfather of Rhode Island governor and U.S. senator Theodore Francis Green and the grandfather of Providence-born George William Curtis, the editor of *Harper's Weekly* from 1853 to 1892 and a noted political reformer of national stature. Burrill's daughter Eleanor married Justice Walter Snow Burges, who is profiled herein.

## U.S. CONGRESSMAN AND CHIEF JUSTICE TRISTAM BURGES

In the estimation of his contemporaries, Tristam Burges was one of the most able Rhode Island attorneys of his era and its greatest debater. This is strong praise for one born into humble circumstances and who received no formal schooling until he was fifteen years of age, though he read voraciously.

Born in Rochester, a small town in southeastern Massachusetts, on February 26, 1770, Tristam was the youngest of the three sons of Abigail and John Burges. His father was a small farmer and a cooper by trade. When Tristam reached his majority in 1791, he became determined to gain a formal education. First, he enrolled at a preparatory academy in Wrentham, where he briefly studied medical-related subjects under the direction of the Reverend William Williams. Leaving Wrentham, he moved to Providence, enrolling at Brown University, from which he graduated in 1796 with highest honors as the valedictorian of his class. For a brief time after graduation, he taught school and studied law. Then, in a stroke of good fortune, he won a lottery prize of $2,000, gave up teaching temporarily and turned his full attention to the practice of law. He was admitted to the bar in 1799 and soon became a formidable trial attorney and a leader of the Federalist Party.

Burges was elected a state representative in 1811 and chief justice of the Rhode Island Supreme Court for a one-year term in 1815. A powerful, eloquent and acerbic speaker, Burges assumed the post of professor of oratory and belles-lettres at Brown in 1815, a chair that had been endowed by Nicholas Brown II, and he taught at the college until 1828. His career as a lawyer and Brown professor was later replicated by his great-great-nephew Theodore Francis Green.

Burges served five terms in Congress from 1825 to 1835 as a National Republican, championing a protective tariff for American industry, serving on various committees

U.S. congressman and chief justice Tristam Burges.

dealing with military pensions and engaging in several famous oratorical duels with the vitriolic John Randolph of Virginia. The issue of slavery gave rise to one alleged exchange between the two masters of rhetorical invective. Randolph once said to Burges, "You pride yourself upon an animal faculty, in respect to which the slave is your equal and the jackass infinitely your superior." Later, hearing rumors that Randolph was impotent, Burges declared that "moral monsters cannot propagate; we rejoice that the Father of Lies can never become the Father of Liars. One adversary of God and man is enough for one universe!"

By the 1830s, Burgess had become a leader of the emerging Rhode Island Whig Party, but in the middle years of this decade, Rhode Islanders supported the Democratic Party of Andrew Jackson and Martin Van Buren. In 1834, Burges was defeated for reelection by Democrats William Sprague II and incumbent Dutee J. Pearce. Prior to 1843, Rhode Island's two U.S. representatives ran at-large because the General Assembly did not divide the state into congressional districts. In the August 1835 contest, Burges polled 125 votes fewer than runner-up Pearce.

The rising, but temporary, popularity of the new Democratic Party of Andrew Jackson ended Burges's political career. In 1836, Jackson's protégé Martin Van Buren carried Rhode Island in the presidential election for the first of only two times the Democrats won the presidential race in Rhode Island during the nineteenth century (the second being the victory of New Hampshire's Franklin Pierce of New Hampshire in 1852). Also in that year, Burges ran for governor as a Whig against four-term Democratic incumbent John Brown Francis. Burges was decisively defeated by a margin of 4,020 to 2,984, despite being the subject of a flattering campaign biography entitled *Memoir of Tristam Burges* by longtime Rhode Island secretary of state Henry L. Bowen. Burges made another attempt for the governorship in 1839 but polled only 457 votes. In 1840, he received 2 token legislative votes for U.S. senator.

Upon his return to private life, Burges resumed the practice of law and commuted to court in Providence from his splendid river-view estate Watchemoket Farm, then in Seekonk, Massachusetts, just across the Washington Bridge, but since 1862 within the bounds of East Providence. His death on October 13, 1853, ended what Rhode Island legal historian Abraham Payne has called a brilliant yet "stormy career." He was interred in Providence's North Burial Ground, at peace at last. Payne, who attended the funeral, described it this way: "It was near the hour of sunset when the door of the tomb was closed, and to apply the words of Theodore Parker, speaking of the death of Dr. [William Ellery] Channing, to the great Rhode Island orator; 'He and the sun went away together.'"

# U.S. SENATOR, GOVERNOR AND SPEAKER WILLIAM SPRAGUE III

The Sprague family is a confusing clan for the historian because there were three William Spragues of note (two are in the Rhode Island Hall of Fame). They were descended from a William Sprague I, a Cranston man of lesser achievements than his successors, though in 1790 he was the one who likely built the simple home that evolved into the present-day Sprague Mansion. The founder of the Sprague textile dynasty, William I, was the husband of Mary Waterman. On June 5, 1773, the couple became the parents of William Sprague II, a farmer and sawmill operator who took up the manufacture of cotton cloth. He introduced the art of calico printing locally, beginning with popular styles known as "indigo blues." In 1808, he built a print works in Cranston near the Pocasset River, around which grew the mill village of Spragueville. William II's marriage to Anne Potter produced two daughters and three sons—Benoni, Amasa and (you guessed it) William III, who was born on November 3, 1799.

Prosperous as a mill owner, in 1821 William II purchased two mills in the Warwick village of Natick and constantly expanded his operations and production. By 1832, he owned 6 percent of all the operating looms in Rhode Island. When he died

U.S. senator, governor and Speaker William Sprague III.

in 1836, he left a budding Rhode Island industrial empire for Amasa and William III to manage. Benoni, the youngest of the three sons, wanted no part of the business operation.

At first, William III was much more interested in using his economic status to gain political power and influence, and at this he succeeded. In his late twenties, he became a state representative from Cranston, and by October 1832, he had gained the office of House Speaker, a powerful post that he held until May 1835. During this tenure, he was the 1832 gubernatorial candidate of the Anti-Masonic Party. In August 1835, he was elected to Congress as a Democrat and served one term before switching parties and defeating the five-term Democratic incumbent, John Brown Francis, in a race for governor.

In 1839, William led in a three-way gubernatorial contest, but he did not secure a majority of the votes cast, as required by law. Because of the deadlock, both for governor and lieutenant governor, first senator Samuel Ward King served as acting chief executive, and William temporarily withdrew from politics to assist his older brother Amasa in the running of the A. & W. Sprague Company, the large textile firm this duo had formed in 1836 upon their father's death.

During the tumult in Rhode Island caused by the so-called Dorr Rebellion, Sprague voted for the People's Constitution in December 1841, but he then became a Law and Order man. His quick change of heart by February 1842 earned him the U.S. Senate seat vacated by the death of Nathan F. Dixon. Sprague's selection was intended to give authority and prestige to the besieged charter government, and it was certainly one that demoralized Thomas Dorr. After supporting the claims of the existing government in the U.S. Senate (in opposition to the claim for legitimacy of Dorr's People's government), Sprague abruptly resigned his Senate seat in January 1844 to return to Rhode Island to lead a police investigation into the December 31, 1843 murder of his brother Amasa.

Sprague's pressure on law enforcement officials led to the hasty indictment and trial of Irish Catholic immigrants John and William Gordon for the brutal crime. John was convicted on the basis of perjured and circumstantial evidence by a biased jury led by a bigoted judge (Job Durfee), and on February 14, 1845, John Gordon was executed by hanging, despite growing popular belief in his innocence. As a result of this miscarriage of justice, Dorr Democrats abolished the death penalty in 1852 after gaining controlling influence in the General Assembly. In 2011, Governor Lincoln Chafee pardoned John Gordon with the advice and consent of the state senate. In an otherwise able analysis of the Gordons' murder trial, entitled *Brotherly Love: Murder and the Politics of Prejudice in Nineteenth-Century Rhode Island* (1993), writers Charles and Tess Hoffman advance the implausible suggestion that William Sprague may have conspired to murder Amasa in order to gain solo control of the family business.

Sprague's final major political achievement was his service as a Whig presidential elector for Zachary Taylor in 1848. Of all the Rhode Island politicians of this formative era, only James Burrill approached Sprague in the importance of the offices he held: Speaker, congressman, governor, U.S. senator and presidential elector. But even in this age of political fluidity, few experienced more changes of heart and political party: National Republican, Anti-Mason, Democrat, Law and Order, Whig and, by the time of his death in 1856, a likely Republican. Surely, William Sprague III would qualify as Rhode Island's premier political chameleon. One might even say that he had the cleanest mind of any local politician because he changed it so often!

In business, however, Sprague was single-minded, aggressive and stayed the course. During the twelve years that he was the sole head of A. & W.

Sprague (1844–56), he presided over the rapid development of a huge textile and real estate empire. By the time of his death, he had expanded the business by constructing large mills in Coventry at Quidneck and in the Pawtuxet Valley village of Arctic (now in West Warwick). In addition, he bought the Rhodes Mill in Natick in 1852 and built the massive (68- by 954-foot) Baltic Mill on the Shetucket River, north of Norwich, Connecticut, and enlarged the Cranston Print Works to make that original facility one of the largest calico-printing factories in the world. Sprague also acquired controlling interest in several banks; he became a leading promoter of the Hartford, Providence and Fishkill Railroad, which connected Rhode Island by rail to the Hudson River in 1854; and he acquired huge landholdings, including Rocky Point in Warwick. By the mid-1850s, he had become the undisputed king of Rhode Island's industrialists.

Unfortunately, his sudden death on October 19, 1856, just short of his fifty-seventh birthday, ended his meteoric run. His son Byron, together with his late brother Amasa's sons—Amasa and William IV—then assumed direction of the Sprague textile and real estate empire.

Sprague's nephew William IV (1830–1915) became the state's "boy governor" in 1860 at the age of twenty-nine, raised a Civil War regiment at the outset of the conflict and served as Rhode Island's United States senator from 1863 to 1875. Before the expiration of his second term, the mighty Sprague empire, much more far-flung and diverse than in 1856, crumbled in the national economic panic of 1873. Most of its textile holdings were acquired by Providence entrepreneurs Benjamin and Robert Knight, whose Fruit of the Loom trademark embraced twenty-one mills by 1896. Ironically, Robert Knight had begun his career in textiles at the age of eight as a worker for the Cranston Print Works in the employ of William Sprague II.

## U.S. Senator and Governor Philip Allen

Philip Allen, older brother of Zachariah by ten years, was born in Providence on September 1, 1785, the son of Nancy Crawford and Captain Zachariah Allen, a prosperous Providence merchant who traded in the Caribbean. Philip received his early education from tutors and in local private schools, and in 1799 he entered Brown University (then Rhode Island College), graduating in 1803. His family connections led to his appointment in 1806 as a director of the Providence Insurance Company; his father, Zachariah Sr., had been one of the first subscribers to this new firm in 1800, a year prior to his death.

U.S. senator and governor Philip Allen.

In January 1814, Philip married Phoebe Aborn, in a union that produced eleven children.

Because of restrictions on commerce imposed by the administrations of Thomas Jefferson and James Madison in an unsuccessful attempt to gain respect for American maritime rights short of war, Philip Allen and other Rhode Island merchants turned increasingly to manufacturing for the domestic market. In 1812, at the outbreak of war, Allen began a career as a textile manufacturer, but he did not achieve major success until 1830, when he established a large calico print works in Providence on Dryden Lane off North Main Street.

Originally named the Woonsocket Company Print Works, the plant was later acquired by Philip's son Crawford in 1857 and incorporated as the Allen Print Works in 1871. Philip was known as an innovator in the operation of his mill. His company owned the first Boulton-Watt low-pressure steam engine built in Providence and was reputedly the first American textile firm to import the improved English bobbin and fly frame. Only the Spragues exceeded Allen in calico production.

Many of the employees of Allen's calico plant were Irish Catholic immigrants. Allen showed his appreciation for their labor by donating two of the three bells he acquired from a Spanish convent for installation in Providence's first two Catholic churches: Saints Peter and Paul (1838) and St. Patrick's (1842). A cynic might say that a grateful workforce is a productive one, but it appears that Allen's generosity was more altruistic. The third bell was placed in the tower of his calico mill, within earshot of St. Patrick's Church.

Allen's career not only embraced commerce, insurance and manufacturing, but it also extended to banking. From 1827 to 1836, when the charter of the Second Bank of the United States expired, Allen was president of that institution's Rhode Island branch.

Unlike his rival, William Sprague III, Allen concentrated on business before indulging in politics, although he served in the General Assembly from 1819 to 1821 as a Providence representative. During Rhode Island's great political upheaval, the Dorr Rebellion, Allen strongly opposed his nephew Thomas Dorr's radical and forceful effort to reform state government, as did Dorr's own father, Sullivan Dorr, and Dorr's brother-in-law, Samuel Ames. The resentment created by such opposition was very slow to heal.

In 1851, Dorr Democrats, the urban reform wing of the party, sought out Allen to head their party's statewide slate. In a tightly contested election, Philip defeated the Whig candidate Josiah Chapin by a margin of 6,935 to 6,106, and the Dorrites gained strength in the General Assembly. Allen won two more annual terms by an increasingly comfortable margin, and in the 1853 balloting, the Democrats gained control of both houses of the legislature for the last time until the Bloodless Revolution of 1935.

During this brief ascendancy of the reform Democrats, a secret ballot law was enacted, the death penalty for crimes was abolished, the number of state capitals was reduced from five to two (Providence and Newport), Dorr was restored to his civil rights and his treason conviction was "reversed and annulled by order of the General Assembly." On May 4, 1853, shortly after Allen's third gubernatorial victory, the legislature in Grand Committee elected Allen U.S. senator "by vote *viva voce, Nem. con*," retroactive to March 4, 1853. Such unanimity in the aftermath of the Dorr Rebellion was very unusual. Allen certainly profited politically from the strong support he received from his nephew's followers, as well as from the votes of those rural Democrats who returned temporarily to the fold until they became alarmed by the scope of reforms advocated by their urban, working-class brethren and found refuge in the Republican Party. However, the extent of the personal rapprochement between the reformer and his uncle prior to Dorr's death in December 1854 remains a matter for speculation, and it is certain that the veto-less Governor Allen was less reform-oriented than the Dorrites who supported him.

As a freshman senator in a house divided, Allen was not very influential during his single six-year term in office. He generally supported the policies of Presidents Franklin Pierce and James Buchanan, but he expressed opposition to the repeal of the Missouri Compromise, looked with disfavor on the Kansas-Nebraska Act of 1854 and voted for protective tariff schedules. Ironically, this prominent textile industrialist from the nation's most urbanized state was entrusted with the chairmanship of the Senate Committee on Agriculture in the Thirty-third and Thirty-fourth Congresses. Cotton, both an agricultural and an industrial commodity, was probably the key that explains this seeming incongruity.

By 1859, Allen had ended his political career and scaled back his business activities. He was succeeded in the Senate by Republican Henry Bowen Anthony. As a textile magnate, Allen's disillusionment with the Civil War was profound. He died in Providence at the age of eighty on December 16, 1865, and was laid to rest in Providence's North Burial Ground only a few hundred yards distant from his famous calico print works.

## U.S. CONGRESSMAN AND JUSTICE ELISHA REYNOLDS POTTER JR.

Elisha Reynolds Potter Jr. was the son and namesake of a very influential and powerful father who could qualify for Hall of Fame status except for his narrow political focus and his unenlightened stands on reform issues. The senior Potter, a practicing lawyer, was a state representative from South

Kingstown to the General Assembly (whose great power he championed) for over three decades, serving five years as its Speaker, and he won four terms in Congress (in 1796–97 and from 1809 to 1815) as a Federalist.

Elisha Jr. was more refined, benevolent and humane than his forceful, outspoken and physically imposing father—and far more likeable. Born at the Potter homestead on June 20, 1811, he was the eldest of five Potter children, and he must have favored his mother Mary (Mawney) Potter in temperament.

U.S. congressman and justice Elisha Reynolds Potter Jr.

Elisha Jr. attended Kingston Academy in his native South Kingstown village of Little Rest (called Kingston since 1825). His homestead was an easy stroll to the Washington County Courthouse. Built in 1775–76, the courthouse was one of Rhode Island's five early statehouses from the era when the General Assembly rotated its sessions among the five counties, thus giving Rhode Island five state capitol buildings, all of which survive in restored condition.

Young Elisha graduated from Harvard College in 1830 and soon began to follow in the footsteps of his father, who had made a political transition from Federalist to Democrat because the latter party was more agrarian-oriented. Throughout their careers, both Potters championed the interests of Rhode Island's rural and agrarian towns. Elisha Jr. became a practicing lawyer in 1832 and was soon a political confidant of Democratic governor John Brown Francis, a relationship he maintained for many years. He also taught the classics at Kingston Academy and began to research the history of South County. In 1835, he published an impressive, still valuable book entitled *Early History of Narragansett*, based on a wide range of primary seventeenth-century materials including deeds, land surveys, agreements with the Narragansett tribe, documents pertaining to Connecticut's claim to the area and family genealogies. In this work, Potter showed great sympathy toward the plight of the Narragansetts.

In 1835, the twenty-four-year-old scholar received an appointment that seems totally out of character when he was named to serve one term as adjutant general of Rhode Island. His father, who died that same year, was far more fitted for such a post. John Brown Francis undoubtedly played a key role in the making of General Potter. Later in the decade (1838–40), Elisha represented his town in the General Assembly.

When the Dorr Rebellion erupted in Rhode Island in 1842, Democrat Potter (like most rural Democrats) sided with the so-called Law and Order Party, which continued to operate under the provisions of the antiquated Royal Charter of 1663. To bolster the position of that faction, he wrote the most learned and balanced criticism of Thomas Wilson Dorr's doctrine of popular constituent sovereignty, a theory that held that the people in their original capacity could bypass a recalcitrant legislature and call their own constitutional convention to change the existing political order. Potter entitled his treatise *Considerations on the Question of the Adoption of the Constitution and the Extension of Suffrage in Rhode Island.*

This effort, along with his role as part of a three-man delegation to Washington, D.C., seeking federal intervention to quell the Dorr Rebellion, his position as state senator and his active leadership in the fall 1842 Law and Order convention that drafted the new state constitution, led to his election to Congress in August 1843 as the first U.S. representative from the state's new "western" congressional district. His victory was due to the support of the Law and Order coalition that consisted of rural Democrats and the dominant urban Whigs. In 1845, when the Law and Order Party split over the issue of Dorr's liberation from prison, Potter was defeated for reelection by the liberation candidate Lemuel H. Arnold. However, Potter had stayed in Washington long enough to vote for the annexation of Texas, a position unpopular with Rhode Island's antislavery Whigs.

At the conclusion of his brief congressional career, Potter served a term in the Rhode Island Senate and turned his energies to the cause of educational reform by assisting the state's first education commissioner, Henry Barnard, to set uniform standards for public schools and implement other educational innovations. When Barnard left Rhode Island in 1848 for new challenges, the General Assembly named Potter his successor. In that capacity, the learned politician from Kingston could share his knowledge and enthusiasm for history, the classics, languages and even agriculture with all Rhode Islanders. To create interest in his efforts, he began the publication of the *Rhode Island Educational Magazine* in 1852, and for its first year he was its main contributor.

The rise of virulent nativism in Rhode Island and in the nation in the mid-1850s hastened Potter's retirement as commissioner, but not before he took two courageous stands on behalf of tolerance. Questions of Bible reading in the public schools and government aid to Catholic schools became burning national issues when the volatile Archbishop John Hughes of New York demanded separate Bibles for Catholic students in public schools and financial aid to church institutions. The spinoff from this New York affair was felt in Rhode Island in 1853, when John Coyle, who taught at St. Patrick's Parish in Providence, advanced these demands locally.

The question of financial aid, of course, received no hearing, but Potter, as state commissioner of education, stated that it would be inconsistent with the state's religious heritage not to allow Catholic schoolchildren the use of their own version of the Scriptures. In a report entitled *Bible and Prayer in Public Schools*, Potter contended that "the reading of the Bible or conducting other devotional exercises at the opening or closing of schools is neither forbidden nor commanded by law, and rests with the teacher, who should respect his own conscience and the consciences of his pupils and their parents." This enlightened view was not held by many, and the intolerant majority continued to demand that the Protestant Bible be exclusively retained.

Opponents of Catholic education also used the truancy device to combat the growth and influence of parochial schools. In 1853, two bills dealing with truancy were introduced into the Rhode Island legislature. The proposed legislation empowered towns and cities to provide by ordinance for the punishment of truant children between the ages of five and fifteen. Under the terms of these measures, successfully opposed by Commissioner Potter, students not attending *public* schools would be regarded as truants and subjected to disciplinary action. Potter resigned as commissioner in 1854 as the Know-Nothing Party gained control of state government, but not before he set in motion an effort to establish a state normal school for the training of teachers, an effort that finally succeeded in 1871 with the creation of a state normal school that has evolved into present-day Rhode Island College.

Unlike many rural Democrats, Potter did not embrace the newly emergent Republican Party, probably because of its nativistic orientation and its antislavery platform that threatened the Union. In 1858, and again in 1859, he was the Democratic candidate for governor. In his first run, he was soundly beaten by incumbent Elisha Dyer (7,934 to 3,572), and in the second effort he was trounced by the relatively unknown Thomas G. Turner (8,938 to 3,536). Potter's role in the Law and Order faction during the Dorr Rebellion cost him the support of urban Democrats.

Undaunted, Potter remained personally popular in South Kingstown, whose voters returned him to the state senate from 1861 to 1863. At that time, and until 1928, each Rhode Island town, regardless of population, was accorded one seat in that chamber. Then, in 1868, his Law and Order affiliations worked in his favor when the Republican-controlled legislature elected him an associate justice of the Rhode Island Supreme Court, a post he held for fourteen years until his death. By the time of his appointment, he and his siblings had fallen on economic hard times, and he had moved his law practice to Newport with the assistance of prominent New York and Newport attorney William Beach Lawrence.

An analysis of Potter's judicial decisions is beyond the scope of this profile and this book's time frame. His demeanor has been described as gentlemanly and courteous toward litigants (at that time, the Supreme Court was a trial court as well as an appellate tribunal). He served on a three-judge panel in the protracted receivership case of the A. & W. Sprague Manufacturing Company after the Sprague failure in the Panic of 1873. He often dissented from the decisions of the other two justices, showing more solicitude for the firm's creditors as opposed to those who seized the company's assets.

Ever the historian, Potter did honor to his mother's ancestors in 1880 by publishing his *Account of the French Settlement and French Settlers in the Colony of Rhode Island*, the story of the French Huguenot exiles who sought a religious haven in Rhode Island and established the East Greenwich village of Frenchtown in 1686. Despite Potter's judicial chores, he remained active in his community, serving often as moderator of the town meeting and maintaining close ties with the Kingston Academy and the Kingston Congregational Church. His donated book collection became the core of the Kingston Free Library.

On April 10, 1882, while still a sitting justice, Potter died of pneumonia at the age of seventy-one. This life-long bachelor was buried alongside his parents in the family cemetery. His voluminous papers, most of which were preserved by South County historian William Davis Miller, are stored at the Rhode Island Historical Society, where a curator surmised that it "may be the best collection in the holdings of the Manuscripts Division for research on either the Dorr Rebellion or early 19th-century Rhode Island politics." The Potter Homestead in Kingston is also well preserved. It was the childhood home of current Rhode Island author Christian McBurney, whose superb general history of Kingston and South Kingstown is a fascinating and detailed account of the social and political milieu that the Potters influenced for nearly a century.

# Governor Elisha Dyer II

The Roman numeral after the name of Governor Elisha Dyer suggests a family first name scenario similar to that of the Spragues. William III (1799–1856) and William IV (1830–1915) were governors of Rhode Island, as were Elisha II (1811–1890) and Elisha III (1839–1909). One wishes that these prominent families could be more creative with their nomenclature.

Elisha I, the father of the first governor Dyer, had an illustrious Rhode Island ancestry dating back to the coming of William and Mary Dyer to Portsmouth in 1638 as exiled disciples of Anne Hutchinson. Mary (profiled in *Rhode Island's Founders*) later espoused Quaker beliefs, and because she defiantly and repeatedly returned to Boston to preach her doctrines, she was executed by order of the Massachusetts Bay Colony's magistrates in 1660.

Elisha Dyer I, born in Glocester on January 5, 1772, became a very successful Providence commission merchant and textile manufacturer. He established two mills along the Woonasquatucket River: the Providence, Bleaching, Dyeing and

Calendering Company on Valley Street in Olneyville and the Dyerville Mill on Manton Avenue in what was then the town of North Providence. He also operated a general commission business on South Water Street in Providence.

Governor Elisha Dyer II.

Elisha Dyer II, the subject of this essay, was a man of diverse talents and interests. After an early education at private schools, he entered Brown in 1825 and graduated in 1829. Two years later, he became his father's junior partner in the commission merchant business, and in 1835 this father-and-son team established the Dyerville Mill to produce cotton cloth. They ran this business jointly until the death of Elisha I in 1854.

In the year the Dyers founded their mill, Elisha II began a lifetime association with the Rhode Island Society for the Encouragement of Domestic Industry, eventually serving as its president from 1859 to 1878. In the late 1830s, he became active in the affairs of the Whig Party, and when the Whigs gained firm control of state government in 1840, Elisha II was elected adjutant general of Rhode Island, a post to which he was reelected for five successive one-year terms. In this position, Dyer played a major role in directing the military maneuvers of the Law and Order government during the Dorr Rebellion.

During the 1840s and '50s, Dyer held leadership positions in an array of civic agencies, both private and public. These included (in part) membership in the Providence School Committee, the presidency of the Fire Wards in the city of Providence, membership in the Butler Hospital Corporation, the presidency of the Providence YMCA, the vice-presidency of the Providence Art Association and the presidency of the Exchange Bank. In 1851, he was the unsuccessful Temperance Party candidate for mayor of Providence. During this time, he remained a dedicated official of the Whig Party organization, but as that party disintegrated during the sectional crises of the 1850s, he moved into a leadership position in the newly emergent Republican Party.

In 1857, Dyer became Rhode Island's first Republican governor, defeating Democrat Americus V. Potter by a decisive margin of 9,581 to 5,323. After outpolling well-respected Democrat Elisha R. Potter Jr. by a vote of 7,934 to 3,572 in 1858, Dyer declined to run in 1859. As he left office, the *Providence Post*, a leading Democratic newspaper, offered an admission: "We have from the first looked upon him [Dyer] as an honorable, high-minded opponent and a straightforward, conscientious man; and candor compels us to say that he has never failed to reach the standard set up for him."

Elisha Dyer II lived for more than three decades following his governorship. An 1881 biographical profile states that "Governor Dyer has been an invalid for the last thirty years, and very much of his work has been done under the burden of infirmity and suffering." Perhaps the condition that afflicted him was rheumatoid arthritis, but surviving accounts do not identify his malady. One thing is certain: it did not detract from his drive, nor did it prevent his additional accomplishments. Dyer volunteered for service in the Civil War, serving three months as captain of the Tenth Ward Drill Company of Providence; he invested in several local railroad ventures; and he continued to make numerous public addresses as an elder statesman on such diverse topics as politics, business, education and music. In the last-mentioned field, he was elected president of the first National Music Congress, a gathering held in Boston's Music Hall in 1869. In addition, Dyer was a Rhode Island commissioner to the London International Exhibition in 1871 and an honorary national commissioner to the Vienna Exposition in 1873. He crossed the Atlantic eighteen times during his career and took extensive notes on his travels to Europe.

On October 8, 1839, Elisha II married Anna Jones Hoppin. One of their seven children, Elisha Dyer III, became a governor of Rhode Island, winning three races in 1897, 1898 and 1899. He also gained admission into the Rhode Island Heritage Hall of Fame by compiling a list of achievements to rival those of his father. Elisha III's grandson, noted local artist Hezekiah Anthony Dyer, has also gained Hall of Fame membership, giving the Dyer family four inductees, including Quaker martyr Mary Dyer.

On May 17, 1890, Elisha Dyer II died at the age of seventy-eight. A devout Episcopalian, he remained a strong advocate of temperance throughout his remarkable life. He is buried in Providence's Swan Point Cemetery.

# IV

# THE LEGALISTS

## JUDGE DAVID HOWELL

David Howell had a distinguished legal and academic career that extended from the Confederation era through the Early National period. He was born in Morristown, New Jersey, on January 1, 1747, the son of Aaron and Sarah Howell. He received his early education at Hopewell Academy in Hopewell, New Jersey, a Baptist school established by clergyman Isaac Eaton. Howell then went to the College of New Jersey (now Princeton University), from which he graduated in 1766. He was preceded at both schools by James Manning, who was nine years older than Howell. When Manning became the founding president of the College of Rhode Island (now Brown University), he asked the young and promising Howell to join him as a member of the faculty. The newly graduated Howell came to Rhode Island in 1766 and began his fifty-eight-year association with Brown.

Howell was a brilliant and versatile academician who not only taught but also studied. By 1769, he had been admitted to the bar, earned a master's degree and attained the position of professor of natural philosophy and mathematics. He also taught French, German and Hebrew. Such scholarly versatility was essential because in the early years of the college, Howell and Manning were the only full-time members of the faculty.

When instruction was interrupted in 1779 by the French army's use of the college's facilities for quartering, Howell became more active in the field of law, serving as a local justice of the peace in 1779 and as a judge of the state Court of Common Pleas in 1780. Two years later, he became a Rhode Island delegate to the Confederation Congress, serving in that capacity until

Judge David Howell.

1785, when he was succeeded by his colleague the Reverend James Manning. Howell's tenure was sometimes stormy. As a representative of Rhode Island's mercantile interests, he stubbornly opposed the attempt by Congress to enact the Impost of 1781, a proposed 5 percent national import duty designed to give the general government a degree of fiscal self-sufficiency. Howell's stance so infuriated his congressional colleagues that they attempted to unseat him. Under the provisions of the Articles of Confederation, the impost needed the unanimous approval of all thirteen states, so it never became law.

The significance of Rhode Island's opposition to the impost was later assessed by John Adams, a rather perceptive commentator. In a February 1790 letter to Providence merchant-politician Jabez Bowen during the debate over Rhode Island's ratification of the new Constitution, Adams stated that "the opposition of Rhode Island to the impost seems to have been the instrument which [divine] providence thought fit to use for the great purpose of establishing the present Constitution." By that date, Howell was a Federalist supporter of ratification.

Howell's congressional tenure gave him a broader national outlook, prompting his 1782 letter to Providence merchant Welcome Arnold in which he praised his adopted state: "As you go Southward, Government verges towards Aristocracy. In New England alone have we pure and unmixed Democracy, and in Rhode Island & P.P. [Providence Plantations] it is in its Perfection."

In 1786, the General Assembly, dominated by the newly ascendant Country Party, surprisingly elected Howell to the position of associate justice of Rhode Island's Superior (i.e., Supreme) Court. In this capacity, Howell was one of the five judges who heard the argument of James Mitchell Varnum urging the high court to declare unconstitutional the force act passed by the agrarian-controlled legislature to compel creditors and merchants to accept the state's new issue of paper money or face fines and imprisonment. The court declined to enforce the law on a technicality, and the General Assembly therefore deposed four of the five recalcitrant judges, including Howell, in the 1787 annual election. Howell nonetheless accepted Varnum's theory regarding the power of judicial review and defiantly stated that his "personal view" was that the act, because of its failure to provide trial by jury, "was indeed unconstitutional, had not the force of law, and could not be executed." Amazingly, the resilient Howell secured election as attorney general in 1789, despite the continued dominance of the Country Party, but he was defeated for reelection in 1790.

In February 1789, just prior to becoming attorney general, Howell joined with Moses Brown, Theodore Foster, John Dorrance, Thomas Arnold and other civic leaders to form the Providence Abolition Society, which they formally incorporated in June 1790. Howell was chosen the society's president and Moses Brown its treasurer. In addition to its role as a moral force against slavery, this organization was authorized to bring court suits on behalf of slaves and to assist in prosecuting actions against illegal slave traders. The most famous of the latter was a suit brought against John Brown in 1796 for violating federal anti–slave trade laws. Brown's acquittal weakened the society, as did the fact that, in the organization's own words, slavery was "nearly extinct" in Rhode Island. By 1805, the society had become moribund, despite the continuing efforts of Howell and Moses Brown.

After his failed attempt in 1790 to win reelection as attorney general, Howell resumed his teaching duties at Brown with the title of professor of jurisprudence. Upon the death of his longtime colleague James Manning in July 1791, Howell became Brown's interim president until the Reverend Jonathan Maxey filled the post in September 1792.

During the negotiation of the Jay Treaty with England in 1794, George Washington appointed Howell as a boundary commissioner. Howell's primary task was to assist in determining the true course of the St. Croix River as the international boundary between Maine and New Brunswick.

During the 1790s, Howell divided his talents among law, teaching and college administration, serving as secretary of the Brown corporation from 1780 to 1806. As a practicing attorney, he earned a reputation as a skilled litigator. According to one source, he was a tall man with an imposing presence, "an excellent public speaker and possessed of a brilliant wit."

Howell gravitated toward the emerging Democratic-Republican Party, and in 1801 Jefferson appointed him U.S. attorney for the District of Rhode Island, a position he held for a year. Then, in 1812, Madison selected him as Rhode Island's U.S. District Court judge. Howell served with distinction in this capacity until his death in July 1824 at the age of seventy-seven. During these years, he continued to serve Brown as a member of the school's board of fellows.

Howell's September 1770 marriage to Mary Brown—a daughter of Jeremiah Brown, pastor of the First Baptist Church—produced five children prior to her death in 1801. The oldest, Jeremiah (1771–1822), became Rhode Island's U.S. senator in 1811 as a Democratic-Republican. He gained this post just before the Federalist Party took over the reins of state government, a change that came about because of the economic hardship caused in Rhode Island by the commercial restrictions enacted by the administrations of Jefferson and Madison to force England and France to respect America's maritime rights. Jeremiah did not seek reelection when his term expired in 1817, and he died in 1822, predeceasing his father.

David Howell's daughter, Waitstill, married Providence businessman and philanthropist Ebenezer Knight Dexter, and another daughter, Mary, became the wife of Rhode Island chief justice Samuel Eddy.

Howell's celebrated brilliance was best described by his Brown colleague Professor William Goddard:

> *Judge Howell was endowed with extraordinary talents…As an able jurist he established for himself a solid reputation. He was, however, yet more distinguished as a keen wit, and as a scholar extensively acquainted, not only with the ancient, but with several of the modern languages. As a pungent and effective public writer he was almost unrivaled; and in conversation, whatever chanced to be the theme, whether politics or law, literature or theology, grammar or criticism, a Greek tragedy or a difficult problem in mathematics, Judge Howell was never found wanting.*

Like Moses Brown, William Ellery and Theodore Foster (all profiled in my first biographical volume), David Howell was both a Rhode Island "founder" and a "maker."

# JOHN WHIPPLE

John Whipple was the acknowledged leader of the Rhode Island bar during the second quarter of the nineteenth century, and he was certainly the one who made the greatest impression on the United States Supreme Court. He was Rhode Island's foremost constitutional lawyer.

Whipple was born on October 22, 1784, the son of Samuel and Deborah Jenckes Whipple. His parents, of Welsh ancestry, were descended from Rhode Island's early settlers. After private schooling in Providence, John entered Brown, graduating in the class of 1802. He was befriended at Brown by college president Jonathan Maxey and went with him to Schenectady, New York, when Maxey was chosen to head Union College. While in New York, Whipple studied law in the office of Henry Yates, a graduate of Yale. Then, upon returning to Providence, he clerked with Samuel W. Bridgham, who would become the city's first mayor in 1832. In 1805, Whipple gained admission to the Rhode Island bar.

One of Whipple's principal areas of litigation involved issues related to Rhode Island's emerging industrial order, and manufacturers occasionally

John Whipple.

called on him to present their case for beneficial business legislation to the General Assembly and the U.S. Congress. His exhortations to the state legislature, in which he sometimes represented Providence, were particularly effective. As a mentor, Whipple presided over the apprenticeship of many Rhode Island lawyers, including Thomas Wilson Dorr. According to the historians of the nineteenth-century Rhode Island bar, Whipple "had a powerful mind, fully conscious of its own strength, and, when speaking, secured the close attention of court, jury, and audience...Almost always there was a large attendance of spectators in court, and when it was known that Mr. Whipple...was to speak, the courthouse would be crowded."

Despite his occasional stints in the General Assembly, Whipple was not greatly involved with elective politics, although he did receive twenty of the ninety-nine Grand Committee votes for U.S. senator in 1851, making him the runner-up in the balloting to the victorious Charles J. James. However, Whipple was pronounced in his political opinions as an avowed admirer of Alexander Hamilton and the Federalist political tradition. Later, this staunch political and social conservative embraced the Whig Party.

Whipple made several appearances before the United States Supreme Court, and he was so effective that Daniel Webster, one of this era's great advocates, regarded Whipple and Jeremiah Mason of New Hampshire as the two most formidable attorneys he had encountered during his four decades of Supreme Court practice. Whipple and Webster had a mutual admiration, as indicated by a treatise that Whipple wrote in praise of Webster.

Whipple's two most notable Supreme Court appearances involved his successful defense of the Rhode Island system of government established by the Royal Charter of 1663. In *Wilkinson v. Leland*, 27 U.S. 627 (1829), Whipple successfully protected the Rhode Island legislature's vast power. Pitted against Webster, he persuaded the high court that the federal guarantee to each state of a republican form of government in Article IV, Section 4, of the federal Constitution did not apply to the doctrine of separated powers, a system that did not exist in Rhode Island. The exact point at issue was the constitutionality of a special state statute, enacted in 1792 pursuant to a private petition to the General Assembly, which in effect validated a void deed. In defending the legislature's action, Whipple unequivocally informed the Supreme Court that Rhode Island's General Assembly "always has exercised supreme legislative, executive, and judicial power," and "it is the best court of chancery in the world." Evidently, the Supreme Court at least acquiesced in this bold assertion of power. Justice Joseph Story, writing for a unanimous court, upheld Rhode Island's General Assembly:

*But it is said that this is a retrospective act, which gives validity to a void transaction. Admitting that it does so, still it does not follow that it may not be within the scope of the legislative authority, in a government like Rhode Island, if it does not divest the settled rights of property.*

Twenty years later, Daniel Webster, the losing counsel in *Wilkinson*, would join Whipple in defending the Rhode Island system of government in the landmark Supreme Court case of *Luther v. Borden*, 7 How. I (1849). When "the God-like Daniel" could not persuade the United States Supreme Court that the power of Rhode Island's legislature was excessive or un-republican, he became a convert.

In the *Luther* case, Webster and Whipple, pitted against the formidable duo of Benjamin Hallett and future associate justice Nathan Clifford, convinced the Supreme Court that it should not rule in favor of the legitimacy of the People's Constitution as implemented in 1842 by Thomas Wilson Dorr and his associates but should reaffirm the legitimacy of the existing Law and Order regime. In a five-to-one opinion handed down in January 1849, Chief Justice Roger B. Taney accepted the main points of the Whipple-Webster argument. The Luthers, who claimed trespass when agents of the allegedly superseded charter government raided their Warren home, had presented a "political question," said Taney, in a conclusion influenced by expedience and practicality. Responsibility to decide questions of disputed sovereignty was not vested with the court but rather with the political branches—Congress and the president, the state legislature and the governor. Taney stated that congressional acceptance of the charter delegation and Dorr's failure to send rival congressmen could be construed as implicit recognition of the Law and Order government. Further, President John Tyler's mere promise of federal support to Governor Samuel Ward King, under the power delegated to the president by Congress to protect states from domestic violence or invasion, was "as effectual as if the militia had been assembled under his orders" said Taney. The Supreme Court, he concluded, would abide by the implicit and explicit actions of the political branches. The doctrine of the "political question," enunciated in *Luther v. Borden*, has remained an important maxim of American constitutional law.

Shortly after this great victory, Whipple retired from the practice of law. According to a colleague to whom Whipple announced his decision, his retirement was "a mistake" because he was "in the full possession of his powers." That same colleague also observed that "Mr. Whipple had faculties not required in the ordinary work of his profession. He was a student of History, a profound thinker on all social, moral, and political questions."

On the personal side, Whipple was twice married, the first time to Maria Bowen of Providence in 1809 and then, after her death, to Ellen DeWolf in 1839. During the last few years of his long life, Whipple often spent quiet time at his country residence in Warwick. He died in Providence on October 19, 1866, at the age of eighty-two. Ellen and a son and daughter by his first marriage survived him, as did his very accomplished cousin Frances Whipple McDougall, who is profiled herein as a member of the Rhode Island Heritage Hall of Fame.

# JOSEPH K. ANGELL

Joseph K. Angell of Providence was one of America's foremost legal scholars of his era. Most of his many legal treatises dealt with changes in the law occasioned by the transformation of the American economy from a commercial to an industrial base, and he was the nation's leading authority on littoral and riparian rights (i.e., tidewaters and watercourses).

Joseph was born on April 30, 1794, the son of Nathan Angell, a storekeeper, and Amy Kinnicutt. He was descended from Thomas Angell, one of the

Joseph K. Angell.

principal associates of Roger Williams in the founding of Providence in 1636. He graduated from Brown University in 1813 in a class that included Zachariah Allen and Job Durfee, and he then studied for the bar at the famous law school run by Tapping Reeve in Litchfield, Connecticut. Upon his return to Providence, he clerked for Thomas Burgess, a future mayor of the city, and gained admittance to the bar in 1816.

After a two-year sojourn in London in a failed effort to establish his claim as heir to an English estate, Angell embarked on a career as a legal theorist and writer of legal treatises. From 1824 onward, he produced a steady stream of books that attempted to address the dramatic transformation in Rhode Island and America from an agricultural and commercial to an industrial economy. His first book, *Treatise on the Common Law in Relation to Watercourses* (1824), examined rivers as a source of power for mills. Angell followed this effort with a series of works that were designed to provide both a history and a summary of legal developments in the forms of business organization and the methods for the transportation of goods. He dealt with the rights of property in tidewaters (1826); actions at law and suits in equity (1829; rev. ed., 1846); private corporations (1834), written with Samuel Ames; state taxation of corporations (1837); eminent domain (1847); the law of common carriers, which he dedicated to his friend John Carter Brown (1849); the law of fire and life insurance (1854); and the law of highways (1857). These works exerted a significant influence on the development of American jurisprudence and were widely praised by contemporary legal scholars, both in America and England.

Angell was concerned with the dissemination of legal knowledge via publication of a monthly periodical, which he entitled *United States Law Intelligencer and Review*, but only three annual volumes appeared before the venture failed in 1831. Because of this effort and his voluminous legal writings, Angell was appointed as the first reporter for the Supreme Court of Rhode Island in the March term of 1845. His summaries of the high court's decisions appeared in pamphlet form in July 1847 and consisted of cases decided as early as 1828, when the court had been reorganized and its justices required to be learned and professional. Angell also prepared a second volume before resigning his reporting position in 1849.

A quiet and scholarly bachelor, Angell generally avoided politics and political controversy, except for his affirmation of Whig principles and his efforts in conjunction with Thomas Wilson Dorr to replace Rhode Island's colonial Royal Charter with a written state constitution. In 1834, he joined Dorr in the creation of the Constitutional Party and assisted Dorr in the preparation of his famous *Address to the People of Rhode Island*, a blueprint for reform presented to the state constitutional convention that met in 1834. Unfortunately, that body was stymied by a conservative majority that resisted change.

Angell continued as a leader of the Constitutional Party until it disintegrated in 1838. However, when the so-called Dorr Rebellion began in 1841, Angell again espoused the cause of reform. He joined with Dorr, Samuel Y. Atwell, Dutee J. Pearce, Thomas Carpenter and four other attorneys in drafting and publishing a treatise entitled *Right of the People to Form a Constitution*. Popularly called "The Nine Lawyers' Opinion," this essay is the most cogent statement of the political ideology at the basis of the People's Constitution. Since called "popular constituent sovereignty," this doctrine held that the people in their primary sovereign capacity can initiate a call for a convention to amend or replace the constitution of a state if change is unreasonably blocked by a reactionary government. Angell, Dorr and their colleagues based their claim on the actions taken during the American Revolution, whereby the sovereign power was divested from the king in Parliament and passed to the people of the colonies without authorization from above. Despite the defeat of the People's Constitution, Abraham Payne, an early historian of the Rhode Island bar, commented in 1885 that he "was not aware that any one of the [nine] lawyers who signed the document ever modified his opinion or doubted its correctness."

On May 1, 1857, the day after his sixty-third birthday, Angell died suddenly in Boston, where he had traveled for business. This scholar, who was described by friends as amiable and "one who died as he had lived—without an enemy," merited a moving eulogy by Chief Justice Samuel Ames, with whom Angell had written a treatise on corporations twenty-three years before.

## Chief Justice William Read Staples

William Read Staples of Providence was a prominent lawyer, jurist and civil servant. With the possible exception of Samuel Greene Arnold, who eulogized him, Staples was also the premier Rhode Island historian of the nineteenth century.

Staples was born in Providence on October 10, 1798, as the youngest son of Samuel and Ruth (Read) Staples. His earliest schooling was with Oliver Angell, who taught at the elementary school level in Providence for nearly a half century. Having completed college preparatory studies at University Grammar School, Staples entered Brown, like many of these early state leaders, and he graduated in the class of 1817. After studying law in the office of Judge Nathaniel Searle for two years, he was admitted to the Rhode Island bar on September 21, 1819.

In the 1820s, Staples became a well-respected attorney and then a prosecutor in the office of the attorney general. In that public post, his most notable assignment was as chief prosecutor in the infamous Avery Murder

Trial of 1833. Unfortunately for Staples, the Reverend Ephraim Avery was acquitted for the savage murder of Tiverton mill girl Sarah Cornell, an acquittal that was regarded, then and now, as a miscarriage of justice.

Despite this setback, his learning and legal skill earned Staples the position of associate justice of the state Supreme Court in 1835. He served in that capacity until 1854, when he was elevated to the chief justiceship. Allegedly for reasons of health, he resigned that post in 1856 to accept an appointment from the legislature as the state's first auditor general.

Chief Justice William Read Staples.

Although law was his profession, history was Judge Staples's great passion. He was an incorporator of the Rhode Island Historical Society (established in 1822) and its first secretary and librarian. His first major published work was a critical edition of Samuel Gorton's *Simplicity's Defense Against Seven-Headed Policy* (1835), describing the early history and travails of Warwick. This book was followed in 1843 by a detailed history of his city—*Annals of the Town of Providence*—which covered events from the original settlement by Roger Williams to the establishment of a city government in 1832, an event in which Staples played a leading role as a member of the first city council.

These productions were followed by a *Documentary History of the Destruction of the* Gaspee (1847), an annotated bicentennial edition of the colony's famous 1647 code of laws (1847), a history of the criminal law of Rhode Island (1853) and the valuable and voluminous history of Rhode Island's ratification of the federal Constitution, entitled *Rhode Island in the Continental Congress* (1870), a posthumously published work that was the basic reference on Rhode Island's entrance into the American Union until it was superseded by the completion in 2012 of the three Rhode Island volumes in the Center for the Study of the American Constitution's massive series entitled *The Documentary History of the Ratification of the Constitution.*

Staples's first marriage was tragic; his two children died very early, and his wife, Rebecca Power, died on September 14, 1825, after only four years of marriage. Staples rebounded quickly, as many in those days seemed to do. In October 1826, he married Evelina Eaton from Framingham, Massachusetts, who gave Staples eleven children. His religious life seemed to be influenced by his spouses. As a youth, he was a Baptist; during his first marriage, he attended services at St. John's Episcopal Church; and then he became what one source has described as "a devout worshiper at the meetings of the Society of Friends."

After his retirement from the Supreme Court, Staples served for a dozen years as the secretary-treasurer of the Rhode Island Society for the Encouragement of Domestic Industry, presided over by Elisha Dyer II. On October 19, 1868, nine days after celebrating his seventieth birthday, Staples died suddenly of a heart attack.

## CHIEF JUSTICE AND SPEAKER SAMUEL AMES

Samuel Ames of Providence served in many public capacities, including state legislator, Speaker of the House, and quartermaster general of the state militia. However, his most memorable service was as chief justice of the Rhode Island Supreme Court from 1856 to 1865.

Ames studied at Phillips-Andover Academy and graduated from Brown University in 1823. He read law for two years under the direction of Samuel W. Bridgham, Providence's first mayor, and studied for a year at the famous Litchfield Law School in Connecticut. Ames was both a successful lawyer and a legal scholar. In 1832, he coauthored the book *Treatise on the Law of Private Corporations Aggregate* with Joseph K. Angell. This work went through ten editions and became a standard authority on private corporate law.

Ames mixed law with politics. As a staunch Whig, he served a decade in the Providence City Council (1841–51) and spent some time as a state representative, becoming Speaker of the House in 1844 and 1845. During the Dorr Rebellion, Ames was a leading member of the Law and Order faction and served as quartermaster general of the state militia that vanquished Dorr. His role in that controversy was ironic in that he had supported Dorr and Joseph Angell in the constitutional reform movement of 1834 and had married Mary Throop Dorr, sister of the famed reformer, in 1838.

On June 26, 1856, the Grand Committee of the General Assembly elected Samuel Ames chief justice of the state's Supreme Court as the successor of William Read Staples. He served in that capacity until five weeks before his death in December 1865. He rendered his most notable opinion in the case of *Taylor v. Place* (1856), a landmark decision asserting the independence of the judiciary from the General Assembly. In this case, Ames declared unconstitutional (under the basic law of 1843) a special act of the legislature setting aside a verdict for Taylor reached by the Providence County Court of Common Pleas in a suit for the recovery of debts. This decision barred a legislative practice that had been commonplace since 1663.

Chief Justice and Speaker Samuel Ames.

Contrary to popular opinion, however, the *Taylor* ruling did not fully embrace the separation of powers doctrine because it left the executive branch subservient to the General Assembly. As Ames stated in his ruling, "However great the *personal influence* of him who, from time to time may fill the executive chair of the state, may be, from his character and standing, his *official power* under our constitution amounts to nothing" (emphasis in original).

Ames's view of the judicial power was much different. Since his *Taylor* decision is the most important ruling in the history of the Rhode Island judiciary and earned for Ames the soubriquet the "Great Chief Justice," and because it reveals the Whig ideology at the basis of Rhode Island's 1843 constitution, it is worthy of extended analysis.

In *Taylor*, the chief justice was influenced by several predictable factors in singling out the judicial branch for emancipation from legislative control. All of these factors were rooted in the work of the Law and Order convention that drafted the state constitution and placed the judiciary on a much different footing than the executive. Although the position of governor was created by the Royal Charter of 1663, until May 1843 the state Supreme Court was purely statutory and a creature of the General Assembly. Clearly, the new constitution had elevated the status of the high court. Secondly, Ames was aware that the Law and Order convention had altered the charter government's Freemen's Constitution of March 1842 by deleting from its Article IV, Section 10, the provision that "the general assembly shall continue to exercise the judicial power." This purposeful omission was a clear indication that the Whig-dominated convention had reservations concerning the legislature's exercise of revisory or chancery powers in judicial proceedings.

Ames may have also received a cue from the name given to the high court in the Law and Order constitution: the "Supreme Court." From 1798 to 1843, the court operated as the Supreme *Judicial* Court, a name that implied that there existed a nonjudicial court—namely, the General Assembly—with review and revisory powers over the judicial court. This, in fact, was how the system worked.

Ames also believed that the grant of judicial power was unlimited but that the governor's power in Article VII, Section 1, was qualified by the word "chief" rather than "sole." He also took judicial notice of the fact that the 1842 convention had used the federal Constitution as a model in crafting Rhode Island's article on the judiciary. "This pregnant sentence ['The judicial power of this state shall be vested in one supreme court, and in such inferior courts as the general assembly may, from time to time, ordain and establish'] is copied into our constitution verbatim from the constitution of the United States," where it has "a settled constitutional meaning," asserted Ames.

Finally, as an orthodox Whig, like the dominant delegates to the Law and Order convention, Ames looked to the judiciary as a bulwark against a Jacksonian-style executive and leveling democracy and as a protector of property rights and societal order. Here he was of one mind with Chancellor James Kent, Justice Joseph Story and such prominent Whig attorneys as Daniel Webster and John Whipple.

For a Whig constitution to empower the judiciary and enfeeble the executive made perfect sense to Chief Justice Ames. His liberation of the Supreme Court was no leap of faith. In the immediate aftermath of a three-year reign of Dorr Democrats (1851 to 1854) who had tried to convene a constitutional convention and liberalize suffrage, who had passed a spate of populistic legislation and who had the boldness to reverse the Supreme Court's verdict in Dorr's treason trial, Ames sought refuge. He found it in an independent court—one that could resist the popular tumult that threatened the governmental structure created by his fellow Whigs in the aftermath of the Dorr Rebellion. In that shelter, there was no room for a dynamic Jacksonian executive.

During his ten-year career as Rhode Island's chief judicial officer, Ames dramatically upgraded the system of reporting court opinions, acting himself as a court reporter. Although he strongly asserted judicial power, he believed that the judiciary should use that power sparingly whenever it evaluated the constitutionality of legislative acts. He was, therefore, an exponent of judicial restraint. One significant interruption of his judicial duties occurred in early 1861, when he served as one of five Rhode Island delegates to the abortive Virginia Peace Convention, a well-intentioned but futile effort to avoid Civil War.

Failing health prompted Justice Ames to retire after nine productive years on the bench. He died in Providence on December 20, 1865, shortly after he stepped down. He was survived by his widow, Mary Dorr, four sons and a daughter. Two of his other children had died in infancy.

## JUSTICE WALTER SNOW BURGES

Walter Snow Burges was a native of Rochester, Massachusetts, where he was born on September 10, 1808, to Rhoda Caswell and farmer Abraham Burges. As a youth, he received a quality common school education, followed by study at a private academy in Sandwich, Massachusetts. Then, his uncle, Congressman Tristam Burges, a former Rhode Island chief justice, oriented Walter toward Rhode Island and Brown University, where Tristam was a professor of oratory and belles-lettres.

Walter graduated from Brown with honors in 1831 and then taught school for four years at Thaxter Academy on Martha's Vineyard while studying law. He was admitted to the Rhode Island bar in 1835 and soon became prominent in his new profession. In 1836, he married Eleanor Burrill, daughter of former U.S. senator and chief justice James Burrill Jr. She bore him three daughters prior to her death in 1865.

Burges became a close associate of Thomas Wilson Dorr; both had Whig Party affiliations in the 1830s. During the Dorr Rebellion, Burges was more moderate in his actions than Dorr and did not take an active part in the

Justice Walter Snow Burges.

attempted implementation of the People's Constitution, but he nonetheless became one of the reformer's most trusted confidants. He was junior counsel in Dorr's 1844 treason trial and was the only person who was allowed to accompany the convicted governor from the trial venue in Newport to the state prison in Providence.

His career subsequent to the rebellion is most interesting. Burges became federal district attorney for Rhode Island under Democratic president James K. Polk from 1845 to 1849, served in both houses of the General Assembly and won election as state attorney general from 1851 to 1854 and again from 1860 through 1863.

Burges's first stint as attorney general was particularly active and noteworthy. From 1851 to 1854, he was the chief legal advisor to Philip Allen and the Dorr Democrats in the General Assembly. He assisted these legislators in drafting and enacting their reform-oriented measures, including a secret-ballot law, the restoration of Thomas Dorr's civil rights, the legislative annulment of Dorr's conviction, a statute abolishing the death penalty and nine proposed constitutional amendments, three of which were ratified, including Amendment II, which gave the governor the power to pardon.

Burges capped his distinguished legal career when he was selected by a Republican-controlled General Assembly to be an associate justice of the Rhode Island Supreme Court, a post he held from 1868 to 1881.

It was to Burges that Dorr left his voluminous papers and correspondence, detailing the course of constitutional reform in Rhode Island during the 1830s and '40s. Burges entrusted these manuscripts to historian Sidney Rider, who used them to write a masterful history of Rhode Island constitutional development that still remains unpublished among the manuscripts of the Rhode Island Historical Society. Having thus utilized the Dorr Papers and added to them, Rider sold the collection to prosperous Providence businessman Marsden Perry, who donated the valuable collection to Brown University, where they are now stored in the John Hay Library.

During his thirteen-year tenure on the Supreme Court, Burges mentored a younger jurist named John H. Stiness, who later became chief justice and much later was inducted into the Rhode Island Heritage Hall of Fame. In a memorial address following Burges's death on July 26, 1892, Stiness described Justice Burges as belonging to the "self-reliant" class of lawyers who "by a sort of natural apprehension, determine what the law is by seeing what it should be." He was a "jury judge," well versed in criminal law, at a time when the state Supreme Court was also a trial court, and he "had no taste for the duties of the appellate court." Stiness concluded his remembrance of Walter Snow Burges with the following exhortation: "Let us rejoice at the record he has left as a good citizen, a warm-hearted friend, a kind neighbor, a genial companion, a sympathetic spirit, a sagacious man of affairs, a trustworthy counselor, an able advocate, a just judge, and an upright man."

# V

# THE EDUCATORS

## JOHN HOWLAND

Without hyperbole, John Howland can well be called "the father of free public education in Rhode Island." He was born in Newport on October 31, 1757, the fourth of eight children in the family of Joseph and Sarah (Barber) Howland. He was the namesake and fifth-generation descendant of a *Mayflower* passenger who had come to Plymouth in 1620 as an indentured servant and rose to become a leader in Plymouth Colony.

John was home-schooled by his parents and aided in his efforts to read by two Newport clergyman who were friends of his very religious father. At age twelve, he and his family moved to Providence, where he became apprenticed to Benjamin Gladding as a barber and hairdresser.

Howland played an active role in the American Revolution, exploits that he described in his fascinating published *Recollections*. After independence was won, he opened his own hairdressing shop in Providence on North Main Street. On January 28, 1788, he married Mary Carlisle, a great-grandniece of Benjamin Franklin, a man whom Howland admired greatly.

In early 1789, Howland was instrumental in forming the Providence Association of Mechanics and Manufacturers, a group that immediately began to lobby for Rhode Island's ratification of the federal Constitution. Once that goal was achieved, the association began its campaign for free public education, with Howland in the lead.

With the assistance of Attorney General James Burrill Jr., in 1799 Howland organized an educational lobby. This effort induced the General Assembly to pass a free-school act on March 13, 1800, despite opposition

John Howland.

from the country towns. Howland directed his town's efforts to comply with this innovative statute, and Providence appointed its first school committee, with Howland as its dominant voice, in August of that year. On the last Monday of October 1800, the Providence tax-supported public school system, consisting of four schools, held its first session; in attendance were 988 white pupils of both sexes, who were to be "faithfully instructed without preference or partiality."

Passage of the School Law of 1800 did not mandate free schools throughout the state, and except for Providence and Smithfield, the towns refused to implement the act fully and secured its repeal in 1803. Providence maintained its system, however, with Howland serving as an influential school committee member until June 1822 and thereafter as a relentless crusader for the free-school cause until his death.

In the final entry of his autobiographical *Recollections*, Howland noted with great satisfaction that "I did what Roger Williams never attempted or never had a disposition to do. I formed and brought into existence the public schools in this town, which Governor Hopkins once attempted but could not accomplish." This work, he stated, will live "for ages after the world shall have forgotten that such a being ever existed as John Howland."

Howland was referring to the fact that during the seventeenth and eighteenth centuries, Rhode Island's schools were private ventures assisted and sometimes encouraged by the towns but supported mainly by fees charged to those who attended them. Town (i.e., public) aid was limited to such actions as building and leasing schools or furnishing part of the schoolmaster's salary. Governments felt that the primary responsibility for education of children resided with parents, relatives, churches and motivated citizens. At the colony and state levels, educational assistance was limited to approving lotteries to raise money for the construction of school buildings, granting corporate charters for institutions of learning and exempting property used for educational purposes from taxation. Education without taxation was the rule that Howland overcame.

Most of the makers of modern Rhode Island profiled herein lack detailed scholarly studies that scrutinize their motives, methods and achievements, but Howland has his analyst. Professor Francis X. Russo of the University of Rhode Island wrote a 1964 doctoral dissertation on "The Educational Philosophy of John Howland," which reveals the reformer's basic beliefs. Howland demanded a good, tax-supported common education that would provide a practical preparation for useful living and, especially, moral preparation and spiritual enlightenment so that future generations would be ensured "liberty of government and security of property." He was convinced that it was the duty of government to provide education for all children, for unless they were educated, an enlightened citizenry would not exist to provide moral and civic leadership. These were surely good thoughts for a man who lacked a formal basic education (though he did receive an honorary master's degree from Brown in 1835).

Other positions of note held by this self-educated reformer included Providence town auditor, town treasurer, president of the Providence Association of Mechanics and Manufacturers, clerk and deacon of the First Congregational Society and president of the Rhode Island Historical Society.

Howland's work with the historical society was especially noteworthy. He was one of that organization's founders in 1822, and he became its president in 1833 upon the retirement of Governor James Fenner. He led this scholarly organization for the next twenty-one years until his death. Howland was not a trained historian (few in those days were). He might be described, rather, as a collector or an antiquarian who greatly enriched the holdings of the society, and in his 1839 presidential address, he encouraged other Rhode Islanders to do likewise.

John Howland was ninety-seven years of age when he died on November 5, 1854. He and his wife, Mary, had five children who lived to adulthood and eight more who died prior to reaching the age of three.

# Henry Barnard

Henry Barnard was born in Hartford, Connecticut, on January 24, 1811, the son of Betsy Andrews and Chauncey Barnard, a sea captain and farmer. He graduated from Yale in 1830, taught school for a year in Pennsylvania and

Henry Barnard.

then returned to Connecticut to study law. Although he gained admission to the bar in 1834, he never practiced as a lawyer. After a sojourn in Europe, he was elected as a Whig to the Connecticut legislature, and he soon adopted the reform of the common school as his great cause.

In 1838, Barnard was instrumental in the passage of a Connecticut state law establishing a state Board of Commissioners of the Common Schools. He was appointed its secretary and held that post until the board's abolition by Democrats in partisan political battles during 1842. Barnard used his brief tenure to initiate state supervision of public schools. Like his Whig associates, he saw the schools as agencies of moral reform, but increasingly he emphasized the social and leveling role of the public school in a democracy. Schools, he contended, should not be regarded as "common" because they were free but because they were for all, within reach of the poor yet attracting the well-to-do by their excellence.

The dissolution of Connecticut's Board of Commissioners gave the Rhode Island General Assembly the opportunity to implement Barnard's ideas in Rhode Island. To this end, Wilkins Updike, a learned South Kingstown legislator, introduced a bill to assess the status of schools throughout the state. When it passed, Barnard was hired into Rhode Island employment at the rate of three dollars per day.

Although his stay was of less than seven years, Barnard exercised a profound impact on local education. The legislature first appointed him as "agent" of the state, charged with preparing a plan to improve the public school system. Thanks to the pioneering efforts of John Howland; of Brown's president, the Reverend Francis Wayland; and especially of Thomas Dorr, the school committee president in Providence, Barnard's stated objective—to raise the other local systems to the standard of that city—succeeded admirably.

Two years of investigation and numerous presentations to town meetings throughout the state enabled Barnard to draft his encyclopedic *Report of the Condition and Improvement of the Public Schools of Rhode Island*, a study that prompted the passage of the School Law of 1845. This statute, written mainly by the legally trained Barnard, was praised by the great educator Horace Mann (a native of Franklin, Massachusetts) as a measure that would give Rhode Island "one of the best systems of public instruction in the world." The school law crafted by Barnard, with the assistance of Wilkins Updike, marked the beginning of modern public education throughout Rhode Island. His state system of education provided for the post of commissioner to oversee the public schools, a position to which Barnard was promptly appointed. Financing, the resolution of disputes and the approval of teachers would all emanate from the state through the commissioner, who would report to the legislature annually. In effect, the General Assembly became the state school board. The goal of this arrangement was "uniformity in the administration of the system" and accountability.

Barnard's legislation also increased the powers and duties of the towns. With the approval of the commissioner, the towns could establish school districts to tax for the support of their schools, while retaining the right to elect school committees and clearly defining their existing powers of examination, inspection, regulation and suspension. In addition, the towns would be authorized to establish public libraries "for the use of the inhabitants generally," a provision that Barnard regarded as "of first importance."

The new law's regulations relating to teachers were stringent for the times. Quoting the maxim that "As is the teacher, so will be the school," the law required the teacher to obtain periodic certification in order to be paid with public funds. It demanded proof of "good moral character," competence in basic subjects and the ability to govern a school or classroom. The qualifications needed for teaching would include "not only knowledge, but the power to impart that knowledge."

To counter the argument that his state system was expensive, Barnard offered a standard Whiggish response: "It was more economical to educate the young than to meet the later costs of pauperism and crime that resulted from ignorance." Further, Barnard asserted that education would elevate the poorer class. One section of his law affirmed his belief that "the cardinal principle of a system of common and public schools [operates] by placing the education of all children, the rich and the poor, on the same republican platform, as a matter of common interest, common duty, and common right." Such a philosophy meant that no child should be deprived of schooling because of the inability of the parent or guardian to pay the school tax.

A staunch advocate of teacher education, Barnard also sponsored a series of institutes for teachers that led to the establishment in 1854 of the Rhode Island Normal School (now Rhode Island College), a project carried forward after Barnard's departure by his successor, Elisha R. Potter Jr. An excellent elementary school on the college's Providence campus is named in Barnard's honor.

Barnard served as the state's first commissioner of education from October 1845 until 1849. His 1848 annual report to the General Assembly contained a detailed and still valuable history of Rhode Island's public school system to that date. In that year, he published a book entitled *School Architecture* to advance his belief that "schools should be comfortable, pleasant places" conducive to learning.

Barnard was probably induced to return home when Connecticut passed a bill in 1849 creating a state normal school for the training of teachers, since the school's first board of trustees selected him to be its principal, a position the law combined with that of state superintendent of the common schools. Subsequent to his stints in Rhode Island and Connecticut, Barnard held numerous educational posts, culminating in his appointment as the first United States commissioner of education in 1867, a position he held until 1870. During the years from 1855 through 1880, he published the massive and influential *American Journal of Education* and wrote several important books on various aspects of the educational process. He left public life in 1870.

According to Edith Nye MacMullen, Barnard's principal biographer, "it is difficult to depict Henry Barnard, the private person." Barnard was clearly popular with his peers and a person of warmth, but he seemed distant from his family. The Catholic faith of his dutiful wife, Josephine, appears to have been a source of friction. He scarcely referred to his children in his correspondence. Two daughters died in childhood, and his son, a lawyer, passed away shortly after his marriage and the birth of Barnard's granddaughter. His two surviving daughters remained unmarried and cared for their illustrious father until his death in 1900 at the age of eighty-nine in the house where he was born.

# VI

# THE CLERGY

## BISHOP ALEXANDER VIETS GRISWOLD

Alexander Viets Griswold was one of the most prominent American churchmen of the early nineteenth century. He was born in Simsbury, Connecticut, on April 22, 1766, the son of farmer Elisha Griswold and Eunice Viets, a woman of German ancestry. As a young boy, he came under the influence of his uncle Roger Viets, a former Presbyterian who had become an Anglican priest. He went to live with Viets, who taught him the classics, mathematics and much general knowledge. Alexander lost his mentor when Viets, a Loyalist, went into exile in Canada after the Revolution. In 1785, Griswold married Elizabeth Mitchelson; their union produced fourteen children.

For about ten years after his marriage, Griswold farmed, studied law and prepared for the ministry. On October 1, 1795, he was ordained by Samuel Seabury, a former Loyalist who became America's first Episcopal bishop. After nearly a decade of missionary work, he was appointed rector of St. Michael's Church in Bristol in 1804 and soon became both a religious and civic leader in his parish town. Griswold came to Bristol, after rejecting other overtures, at the invitation of William Pearse II, a warden of St. Michael's Church and the principal landowner on Bristol Point. He was transported to this port town on a ship owned by parishioner James DeWolf and piloted by his brother John. Upon arrival, he was greeted by the twenty-five families who then attended St. Michael's.

To increase parish membership, Griswold inaugurated certain "evangelical" innovations, such as evening lectures and services. According

Bishop Alexander Viets Griswold.

to Griswold's autobiography, on the eve of the War of 1812 the people of Bristol exhibited "an awakened attention to the subject of religion," a revival that caused his congregation to grow dramatically. A similar revival occurred in 1820, during which over one hundred persons were confirmed. Such outbursts of religious zeal influenced Griswold to become less formal and more evangelical in his religious demeanor.

While in Bristol, he prepared scores of sermons and lectures, but despite the urging of friends he declined to publish them. However, he did write several devotional books during the course of his career. While at St. Michael's, he also found time to direct the studies of many students in what his biographer calls "the best theological seminary which the Eastern Diocese ever had."

Griswold maintained a close relationship with Brown University, despite its Baptist connections. In 1810, he received an honorary master's of art degree from Brown, followed by an honorary doctorate of divinity in 1811. He was elected to Brown's Board of Fellows in 1812 and was made a "Chancellor of the University" in 1814, an office he held until he moved from Rhode Island. His daughter, Sylvia, married Professor John DeWolf of Bristol, a noted Brown University chemist.

During his twenty-six-year tenure in Rhode Island, Griswold also assumed a leading regional role in the American Episcopal Church. On May 29, 1810, a convention, consisting of delegates from Maine, New Hampshire, Vermont, Massachusetts and Rhode Island, met in Boston to form the Eastern Diocese, the first Episcopal diocese not to be coterminous with one state's boundaries. To his surprise, Father Griswold was elected its bishop, and he was consecrated on May 29, 1811. In addition to his chores in Bristol, from that time onward he also performed missionary work throughout his new diocese. The Eastern Diocese endured until Griswold's death in 1843, making him its first and only bishop. By that time, his diocese had grown from twenty-two churches to one hundred, in part because of his tireless missionary efforts throughout the region on behalf of a schismatic denomination that had emerged due to the American reaction to an Anglican Church whose head was the king of England.

In 1830, Griswold resigned his rectorship at St. Michael's to take the same post at St. Peter's Church in Salem, Massachusetts. After a five-year tenure there, he left to devote himself full time to his episcopacy, having become the fourth presiding bishop of the American Episcopal Church in 1836.

As a religious leader, Griswold exerted a significant influence on his church, both locally and nationally. As a pamphlet writer and a dynamic missionary preacher, he became a leader of the Evangelical wing of the Episcopal Church, a party that opposed the "High Churchmen" and the developing Oxford movement within Anglicanism, because the adherents of such views favored rituals and doctrines that resembled Roman Catholicism. According to one of his biographers, "Griswold molded an Evangelical party that influenced the Episcopal church throughout most of the nineteenth century."

Described by a contemporary as "a man of mighty frame and herculean strength," Griswold outlived his first wife, Elizabeth, who died in 1817, and all but one of his fourteen children. He died of a heart attack in Boston on February 15, 1843. He was first buried beneath the chancel of Boston's Trinity Church, but when that structure was destroyed by fire, his remains were moved to St. Paul's churchyard in Dedham. A mural tablet on St. Michael's Church in Bristol bears an inscription to his memory. One newspaper story about Griswold was effusive in its praise: "The moral influence of such a life is invaluable, and should not be confined to one denomination—it belongs to the world."

## REVEREND FRANCIS WAYLAND

Francis Wayland was a prominent Baptist minister, the president of Brown University from 1827 to 1855, the pastor of Providence's First Baptist Church in 1857 and 1858 and an influential moral philosopher.

Wayland, the son and namesake of a Baptist minister, was born in New York City on March 11, 1796, and graduated from Union College. Then, after two years of medical study, he attended Andover Theological Seminary and entered the Baptist ministry. Wayland's first assignment was as minister of the First Baptist Church of Boston from 1821 to 1826. There he met his first wife, Lucy L. Lincoln, by whom he had three sons prior to her death in 1834. In 1838, he married Hepsy Sage but had no children by his second wife.

As the author of fourteen books dealing with such topics as education, political economy, slavery, evangelical Protestantism and social reform, the conservative Wayland stressed the notion that individual conscience was a reliable guide for action, but only if it were informed by religious training

Reverend Francis Wayland.

and common sense. Such books as *Elements of Moral Science* (1835), a popularly written treatise on personal ethics that went through several editions; *Elements of Political Economy* (1837); and *The Elements of Intellectual Philosophy* (1854) were widely read and very influential in educational circles.

Wayland was not only a college leader, but he was a civic leader as well. As the newly installed president of Brown, he was instrumental in the passage of the state School Act of 1828. After inspecting the Boston school system, he drafted a report that urged the adoption of Boston's structure by Providence, including the gradation of education into three levels—primary, grammar and high school. The first level, for children ages four through seven, would separate "the small scholars from the larger," and according to Wayland's report, instruction in primary schools could be provided by females and the use of a "monitoring system," whereby bright students could assist those who learned more slowly. The 1828 law also elevated the status of school committees from purely advisory bodies to agencies that exercised exclusive control of the school system. Wayland's passion for order prompted him to serve for many years as an inspector of the state prison and the Providence County Jail and as president of the local Prison Discipline Society.

During the Dorr Rebellion, Wayland was an outspoken defender of the existing government. His conservative position was predictable in view of the thesis of his 1838 book on *The Limitations of Human Responsibility*, wherein he insisted on the reformers' need to respect the autonomy of every individual, "however benighted," even if such self-restraint permitted the continuance of wrong. Wayland expressed particular criticism of moral reform associations. True to his beliefs, he denounced the Dorrites in an 1842 treatise entitled *The Affairs of Rhode Island* and delivered a major "discourse" of thanksgiving on July 21, 1842, after Thomas Dorr had fled into exile. For good measure, Wayland published an extensive essay on *The Duty of Obedience to the Civil Magistrate* in 1847, the same year he played a leading role in a local relief effort to assist the famine-plagued people of Ireland. By the 1850s, he was called by some "the first citizen of Rhode Island."

Wayland was an outspoken man with a formidable personality and an imposing, dignified appearance. Rhode Islander James Burrill Angell, of Brown's class of 1849 and later the president of the University of Michigan, remembered that "the discipline of the college was wholly in his hands. In administering it, he was stern, at times imperious. But no graduate of his time ever failed to gain from him higher ideals of duty or lasting impulses to a noble or strenuous life…Hardly a week of my life has passed in which I have not recalled some of his apt sayings, and to my great advantage."

As president of Brown University from 1827 to 1855, Wayland advocated what were then controversial educational reforms: that some courses of study could last less than the traditional four years, that a student be allowed to choose his own courses and that a professor be paid according to how many students studied with him. After years of confrontation with the college's trustees, Wayland resigned his presidency in 1855 and soon assumed the pastorate of Providence's famed First Baptist Church.

As a minister who believed that the measure of a good pastor was not his learning or oratorical skills but rather his evangelical skills, Wayland was well suited for his new post, but he relinquished his pastorate in 1858. Perhaps the highlight of his religious career was his presidency of the General Missionary Convention of the Baptist Denomination in the United States for Foreign Missions, a post he held in 1844–45 and which prompted him to write *Memoirs of Adoniram Judson*, detailing the labors of the famed Baptist missionary to Burma.

Wayland died in Providence on September 30, 1865. He was survived by his wife, Hepsy, and his children, who laid him to rest in the North Burial Ground. His oldest son, Francis Wayland III (1826–1904), was lieutenant governor of Connecticut in 1869–70 and became a professor and dean of the Yale Law School.

# Reverend James Fitton

Father James Fitton was one of New England's foremost and most successful Catholic missionary priests. He was born in Boston on April 10, 1805, the son of Abraham Fitton, a wheelwright, and Sarah Williams, a native of Wales and a convert to Catholicism. James attended pubic schools and a small parish school in Boston, where he began to serve as an altar boy in Holy Cross Cathedral during the episcopacy of Jean Louis Cheverus. Bishop Cheverus encouraged young Fitton to enter the priesthood and sent him in 1822 to study Latin and Greek in Quebec. In 1824–25, Fitton attended a Catholic academy in Claremont, New Hampshire; then he received further theological training from Boston's new bishop, Benedict Fenwick, who ordained Fitton to the priesthood on December 23, 1827.

Father Fitton's first missionary assignment was to the Passamaquoddy Indians of Eastport and Old Town, Maine, whom he later described as "devoted Christians of the forest." In 1830, he was dispatched to Hartford, where he founded Trinity Church in 1831, the first Catholic parish in that community, and where he began to publish a short-lived Catholic newspaper. For the next quarter century, Fitton was ubiquitous. His travels took him literally to every corner of New England, oftentimes on foot, carrying a valise containing vestments, chalice and other essentials for offering Mass in the region's scattered Catholic settlements, usually mill villages populated by Irish immigrants. Along his many routes, he sometimes encountered harassment and hostility from those who regarded him as an emissary of a foreign potentate—the pope of Rome.

Reverend James Fitton.

Fitton's exploits in Rhode Island were far-flung. In 1834, he began regular visits to the Woonsocket area to say Mass for the Irish builders of the Blackstone Canal who settled there. In 1837, he oversaw the construction of Our Lady of Mount Carmel Church (known as St. Mary's) in the Pawtuxet Valley mill village of Crompton.

In October 1843, Bishop Fenwick asked Father Fitton to take over the ministry of Saints Peter and Paul in Providence, where the congregation had divided over such issues as temperance reform, responses to the Dorr Rebellion, the tactics to be employed to repeal the 1801 Act of Union with Great Britain and the allegedly "authoritarian attitude" of pastor John Corry. Fitton succeeded in healing the divisions within the congregation, as well as the animosities that existed between it and the newly established St. Patrick's Church on Smith Hill. As one means of reconciling the various factions in Providence, Fitton joined with Father William Wiley at St. Patrick's to organize a Confraternity of the Blessed Mother, a devotional group that came to embrace the majority of the members of both churches.

While in Providence, Fitton, with the help of his congregation, enlarged Saints Peter and Paul Church and paid off its debt, thus making it suitable for the bishop's residence when the Diocese of Hartford was set off from Boston in 1844. The bishop of the new diocese, Yankee convert William Tyler, chose Providence as the seat of his religious domain and Saints Peter and Paul as his cathedral. When Tyler settled in Providence in 1844, he sent Father Fitton, his trusted seminary classmate, on a new assignment in Newport to put the affairs of St. Mary's Church in order.

Soon, Fitton, who prided himself as a church builder, proposed a more elaborate house of worship for Rhode Island's first permanent Catholic parish. With assistance from the local Irish community and Newport summer resident Mrs. Goodloe Harper, daughter of Charles Carroll of Maryland (the only Catholic signer of the Declaration of Independence), work on this new edifice began. Plans were drawn by the soon-to-be-famous church architect Patrick C. Keely, and Fitton obtained construction assistance from soldiers at Fort Adams under the direction of Lieutenant William S. Rosecrans, a Catholic engineering officer, who later rose to the rank of Union general in the Civil War and came close to being named Abraham Lincoln's 1864 running mate.

Begun in August 1848, St. Mary's, a striking Gothic Revival building, was finally dedicated on July 25, 1852, by Bishop Bernard O'Reilly. Over the years, it has been the setting for many important ceremonies, including the wedding of John F. Kennedy to Jacqueline Bouvier.

Fitton's other major achievement during his missionary years involved the founding of Holy Cross College in Worcester, where he had established that town's first Catholic parish. In 1840, he purchased a site in that town for the education of young men and opened Mount St. James Academy, named for his patron. In 1843, after Fitton transferred the fledgling school to Bishop Fenwick, it was entrusted to the Jesuit Order and became the College of the Holy Cross. Especially before the opening of Providence College in September 1919, many Rhode Island Catholic boys obtained their college educations at "the Cross."

In 1855, at the age of fifty, the restless Fitton came home to Boston to stay. As pastor of an East Boston parish during the next twenty-six years, he continued his earlier practices of preaching, writing pamphlets and translating devotional books and tracts. In 1872, he also compiled an account of his missionary efforts entitled *Sketches of the Establishment of the Church in New England*. In addition, Fitton founded three Boston-area parishes, three literary societies and three parochial schools.

Father Fitton died in Boston on September 15, 1881, at the age of seventy-six. At his passing, this tireless cleric was hailed as "the great missionary of New England." His work in Rhode Island merits the same encomium here.

# Mother Mary Frances Xavier Warde

Mary Frances Xavier Warde was the American foundress of the Sisters of Mercy (RSM). Born in Ireland in 1810 to fairly prosperous parents, she was orphaned in her teens. At age sixteen, she moved to Dublin, where she met Catherine McAuley, a social service worker who established the Sisters of Mercy in 1831 to provide for the education and social needs of poor children, orphans and the sick, as well as homeless young women. Warde immediately joined the new order and became one of McAuley's top assistants.

After establishing several convents in Ireland, Warde migrated to Pittsburgh, Pennsylvania, in 1843 at the request of Bishop Michael O'Connor. Her educational work on behalf of the Irish immigrants in that city prompted Irish-born Bishop Bernard O'Reilly to invite the Sisters of Mercy to Providence in 1851. Although Hartford was named the seat of

Mother Mary Frances
Xavier Warde.

his diocese when it was created in 1844, O'Reilly's predecessor, Yankee convert William Tyler, had chosen Providence over Hartford as the site of the diocesan cathedral.

Bishop O'Reilly's motives for inviting the Sisters of Mercy to his diocese were clear. Faced with a public school system with strong Protestant overtones, he sought an alternative that would provide a Catholic value-oriented education. In addition, he had a special desire to aid the orphans of the diocese who, through the untimely death of their parents or as a result of abandonment, were sometimes placed in Protestant homes. The bishop hoped to build on the work of the Young Catholic Friends Society, founded in Providence at St. Patrick's Parish in 1848 to raise funds to support orphans in Catholic homes and to establish a Catholic orphanage. For this dual purpose—education and social welfare—the Sisters of Mercy came to Rhode Island.

Mother Xavier Warde (the "American foundress") and four sisters arrived in Providence on the evening of March 11, 1851, while Bishop O'Reilly was visiting parishes in Connecticut. Initially, they lived in a small cottage on High (Westminster) Street. Then, in May, O'Reilly purchased the Stead estate at the corner of Providence's Broad and Claverick Streets, along with a frame house on the adjacent lot.

Within a year, the Mercy community had expanded to thirteen. The sisters took over the schools at the Cathedral and St. Patrick's in 1851 and those at St. Mary's (Newport) and St. Joseph's (Providence) in 1854. In addition, they assumed the care of nineteen female orphans in the frame house adjacent to their convent. To support their constantly expanding ministry to the orphans, the sisters instituted an annual Orphan's Fair that received the widespread support of both Catholic and Protestant communities. In 1852, these commendable efforts were extended to New Haven and Hartford, where new orphan asylums were soon opened.

Catholic education, the principal function of the sisters, was also a prime concern of O'Reilly. During the 1850s, the bishop provided the impetus for the expansion of Catholic schools in Rhode Island. His report on education in 1855 was a forerunner of the position that would be officially adopted later in the century by the Vatican's Third Plenary Council. Both he and Warde advocated a school in every Catholic parish.

The entire Catholic community responded to this exhortation. Over the next decade, the Sisters of Mercy undertook the education of most girls in parish elementary schools throughout southeastern New England. Their efforts were augmented by a dedicated group of laymen who taught the boys and young men not forced by family circumstances to work long hours in the factories. Parents also recognized the importance of Catholic education by tolerating the inferior physical plants that passed for parochial school buildings in this early period. This enthusiasm for education manifested by Rhode Island's Catholic community resulted in the establishment by 1860 of seven elementary schools and one female academy, which the sisters initially established in their Providence convent.

There are few enrollment records available for the early Catholic schools. However, the Reverend Americo L. Lapati, the historian of Catholic education in this state, has provided figures on some of the parish units. From his estimates, it appears that the total Catholic school enrollment by 1860 was 1,900. In addition to those formally attending Catholic institutions were the large numbers of children who participated in parish Sunday schools. While O'Reilly labeled these schools "feeble auxiliaries to Catholic education," he recommended their continuance, since funds for building regular schools were lacking and because so many children were employed in factories. Under the direction of Mother Warde and Bishop O'Reilly, Catholic education made a formidable beginning in the years before the Civil War. A firm foundation was established for the great expansion of teaching orders and parish institutions that occurred in later decades.

The quality of education in these first schools compared favorably with that in their public school counterparts. Much of the credit for this condition rests with Mother Warde, one of the foremost Catholic educators of the nineteenth century. Her system of instruction was quite comprehensive compared to present approaches. The typical day consisted of two learning sessions separated by a two-hour break for lunch and recreation. The three-hour morning session and the two-hour afternoon session were devoted to a broad range of subjects that increased as the student reached the academy, or high school, level. At the core of this program was a thirty-minute daily catechism lesson based on the illustration of religious truths by stories and examples rather than mere recitation.

Mother Warde's single most impressive legacy to Rhode Island was St. Xavier's Academy, which opened in 1851, only eight years after Providence inaugurated the state's first public high school. A boarding and day school combined, St. Xavier's served as a novitiate for postulants and as a finishing school for girls of families with sufficient means. It was first housed in the convent on High Street before moving into a newly built brick building on Claverick Street in 1856, the capacity of which was doubled nine years later. St. Xavier's curriculum expanded on the traditional elementary subjects while placing added emphasis on conversational French, basic Latin and the fine arts. Lessons in voice, piano and guitar were included at additional cost. In 1874, the boarding department was transferred to the newly established St. Mary's Academy, Bay View, in East Providence.

Mother Warde's Rhode Island apostolate was highly successful despite intense opposition from anti-Catholic nativists. In March 1855, at the height of the infamous Know-Nothing movement, these zealots threatened to burn the Providence convent of "the female Jesuits" on Claverick Street for allegedly harboring a Protestant girl against her will. The mob was repulsed by Bishop O'Reilly and city authorities. Unknown to the nativistic crowd that gathered in front of the convent, more than one hundred armed Irish workmen had assembled in the garden of the convent. Mother Warde exacted from them a promise that no shot would be fired unless in self-defense. Fortunately, violence was averted. Less than a year after the convent confrontation, the courageous O'Reilly perished at sea in an Atlantic storm as he returned from Ireland, where he had ventured to recruit diocesan priests.

Warde served as superior of the Mercy order in Providence until 1858. She continued her missionary work after her departure from Providence in that year, founding a total of twenty-seven convents in ten states. By the time of her death on September 17, 1884, at Manchester, New Hampshire, she had been responsible for bringing her new order of nuns to the service of thousands of Catholic immigrants from Maine to California. A well-documented and authoritative biography of this great religious missionary is Kathleen Healy's *Frances Warde: American Founder of the Sisters of Mercy* (1973).

In an age when most Americans, including females, believed that a woman's place was only in the home, Catholic religious orders of women ran and taught schools, operated orphanages, administered and staffed hospitals and ministered to the spiritual needs of their coreligionists. To most modern practitioners of so-called women's studies, however, these nuns have remained historically cloistered. Recognition of the pioneering role in American life played by women like Mother Warde is long overdue.

# VII

# The Physicians

## Dr. Solomon Drowne

Solomon Drowne was born on March 13, 1753, in Providence, the son of Mary Tillinghast and merchant Solomon Drowne (whose father and great-grandfather were also named Solomon). Private tutors prepared him for his entry into Brown University, from which he graduated in 1773 with highest honors. He then embarked on a medical career, interning with Dr. William Bowen and earning medical-related degrees from the University of Pennsylvania and Dartmouth College. As a surgeon in the American Revolution, Drowne wrote a journal (published by his descendants in 1872) that detailed his service on the private sloop-of-war *Hope*. After the war, he journeyed to Europe to gain more advanced medical knowledge, and there he gained the acquaintance of several leading European physicians.

The adventurous young doctor next traveled to the virginal Ohio Country with such notable Rhode Island westward pioneers as James Mitchell Varnum, for whom he gave a funeral eulogy after Varnum's sudden death in January 1789. In the next decade, Drowne also took up residence in Morgantown (now in West Virginia) and in Uniontown, Pennsylvania. In 1801, he came back to Rhode Island to stay. Dr. Drowne established a residence in rural Foster, the state's newest town, and continued his lifelong association with lawyer and U.S. senator Theodore Foster (1752–1828), for whom the town had been named when it was set off from Scituate in 1781. Drowne and Foster (whose Senate career concluded in 1803) had been friends from their student days at Brown. Both men were scholars, and both had long talked of establishing themselves in an idyllic rural setting conducive to contemplation and the pursuit of their respective

Dr. Solomon Drowne.

professional interests while still maintaining their professional contacts in Providence.

Drowne's focus became botany and herbal medicine. At his country estate, which he named Mount Hygeia after the Greek goddess of health, he engaged in a number of remarkable experiments that combined his physician's belief that natural remedies were best with a botanist's curiosity in discovering new kinds and qualities of plant life. Drowne cultivated extensive botanical gardens around his north Foster home, growing medicinal plants and herbs and ornamental plants, both native and imported. In addition, he planted many varieties of trees, including the mulberry, which could be used to host silkworms. While carrying on this work, Drowne also served for more than two decades as professor of materia medica and botany at Brown University's first medical school, and he became a popular public lecturer on health-related topics.

Drowne did even more than plant and teach. In 1819, he was a delegate to the medical convention that created the U.S. *Pharmocopeia*, served as vice-president of the Rhode Island Medical Society, wrote numerous treatises and essays on a variety of scientific subjects, was an active member of the American Academy of Arts and Sciences and published, with his son William, the *Farmer's Guide*, a comprehensive work on animal husbandry and gardening. In addition, he took an active part in the organization and proceedings of the Rhode Island Society for the Encouragement of Domestic Industry.

Drowne married Elizabeth Russell, whose brother, Jonathan Russell of Providence, later became a congressman and a member of the five-member American delegation that negotiated the Treaty of Ghent, ending the War of 1812. Solomon and Elizabeth had nine children, six of whom lived into adulthood. He died in Providence on February 5, 1834; she died at Mount Hygeia on May 15, 1844.

For many years after Drowne's death—memorialized by his professorial colleague Dr. Usher Parsons with an 1834 biographical sketch—Mount Hygeia was carefully maintained by his descendants. From 1941 to 1963, however, with the death of Drowne's last direct descendant and ownership disputes among absentee heirs, the estate became vacant and prone to vandalism. Fortunately, the ownership problem has been resolved, and this historic house has now been rescued and restored. The memory of Dr. Drowne's achievements is equally worthy of preservation.

## Dr. Usher Parsons

Usher Parsons was Rhode Island's foremost physician of the early nineteenth century. Born in Alfred, Maine, on August 18, 1788, he was the youngest of the nine children of Abigail Blunt and William Parsons, a farmer and trader. Though he had little formal schooling, he began the study of medicine as an apprentice to a physician in Alfred and then to Dr. John Warren of Boston.

Dr. Usher Parsons.

Parsons was licensed to practice by the Massachusetts Medical Society in 1812, and he immediately gained valuable experience as a surgeon's mate for Rhode Islander Oliver Hazard Perry (see appendix) in the September 10, 1813 naval Battle of Lake Erie. Usher's distinguished naval service brought him not only a medal and prize money but also a promotion to the rank of surgeon and Commodore Perry's praise and friendship.

Parsons's performance in that pivotal battle was extraordinary. Because of a temporary illness afflicting his two associate medics on Perry's flagship *Lawrence*, the whole duty of attending to nearly one hundred wounded men and as many more sick with fever fell squarely on twenty-five-year-old Parsons. In a letter to the secretary of the navy after his famous exultation, "We have met the enemy, and they are ours!" Commodore Perry praised Usher's heroic effort: "Of Dr. Usher Parsons, surgeon's mate, I cannot say too much…it must be pleasing to you, sir, to reflect, that of the whole number wounded, only three have died. I can only say that, in the event of my having another command, I should consider myself fortunate in having him with me as a surgeon."

After several years of naval service, including duty with Perry against the North African pirates and a European cruise on Commodore Thomas Macdonough's frigate *Guerrière*, which gave him the opportunity to meet with several prominent English and French physicians, Parsons earned his MD at Harvard in 1818. He became a professor of surgery and anatomy at Dartmouth College in 1820 for a brief period before coming to Providence in 1822 to assume a professorship at Brown University's short-lived medical school. In that year, Parsons married Mary Holmes of Cambridge, Massachusetts, elder sister of Oliver Wendell Holmes Jr., the eminent poet and father of the noted jurist. Mary died in 1825, leaving Usher with one son, Charles, who also became a prominent physician. Mary's death so devastated Usher that he never remarried.

Dr. Parsons's associates on the Brown Medical School faculty were Dr. Solomon Drowne, professor of materia medica and botany; John DeWolf, professor of chemistry and son-in-law of Bishop Alexander Griswold; and Dr. Levi Wheaton, professor of theory and practice of physic and obstetrics, who also maintained a private practice with Parsons for a short time. Parsons's title, reflecting his major areas of expertise, was professor of anatomy and surgery. The four-man medical school was discontinued in 1827 when Brown's new president, the Reverend Francis Wayland, required full-time service to the university by all professors. According to Parsons's son Charles, "The policy of President Wayland, requiring the officers of instruction to be also officers of discipline and give their whole time to collegiate duties, necessarily severed his [Usher's] connection with the University."

In 1820, Parsons published *Sailor's Physician*, a manual of sea medicine for use on merchant vessels. Retitled *Physician for Ships*, the volume went through four editions and remained a standard work in its field for decades. Dr. Parsons was president of the Rhode Island Medical Society from 1837 to 1839, a founder and president of the Providence Medical Society and one of the organizers of the American Medical Association, serving as its acting president in 1854.

In 1851, while Dr. Parsons was president of the Providence Medical Association, he initiated a campaign to establish a general hospital in Providence. The efforts of that society's hospital committee, which he chaired, were unsuccessful, and the project lay dormant until a bequest for such a facility was made by the will of textile magnate Moses Brown Ives. This gift dramatically revived the project, and in January 1863, twelve Providence physicians, in concert with the Ives family, petitioned the General Assembly for a hospital charter, with Parsons's name heading the list of petitioners. With the charter granted in May 1863, the city of Providence donated land for the new facility on Eddy Street in South Providence that had been the site of a smallpox quarantine station in 1776 and the location of a building constructed in 1797 to house and treat yellow fever patients. Parsons contributed both medical and financial assistance toward the establishment of Rhode Island Hospital. When it opened on October 1, 1868, he became one of its first consulting physicians because, at age eighty, he could no longer perform operations.

Parsons wrote voluminously on medical topics, winning several prizes for his work. He also expounded on other subjects, including the Battle of Lake Erie, the place names and burial sites of Rhode Island's Native Americans and a biography of his maternal ancestor, Sir William Pepperrell, who commanded the British expedition that captured the French fortress of Louisbourg on Cape Breton Island in 1746, during King George's War.

Parsons himself has recently been the subject of a scholarly full-length biography by Dr. Seebert J. Goldowsky entitled *Yankee Surgeon* (1988), and his War of 1812 diary has been edited and published by prominent military historian John C. Fredriksen. Both works are based on the *Memoir of Usher Parsons, M.D.* written by his son Charles in 1872, when Charles was a professor of physiology at Brown.

Dr. Parsons died in Providence on December 19, 1868, at the age of eighty as a result of an apparent stroke suffered on October 17, less than three weeks after his hospital dream was fulfilled. He was attended at home by his physician son, Charles, with whom he lived. His obituary was effusive but accurate: "As a surgeon, his reputation for a long time after coming to the State, was superior to that of any other in the State, and his opinion as well as his skill as an operator, was often sought in difficult cases, both in the city and in all the neighboring county."

In the late 1980s, a real estate partnership consisting of Vincent A. Cianci Jr., Paul Campbell, Fernando S. Cunha and the author built a four-story medical office building at 90 Plain Street adjacent to the hospital campus, naming the building in honor of Dr. Parsons. A subsequent owner removed that designation.

# DR. ISAAC RAY

Dr. Isaac Ray was one of the fathers of American psychiatry. Born in Beverly, Massachusetts, on January 16, 1807, he was the son of Captain

Isaac Ray and his second wife, widow Lydia Symonds. Ray graduated from Phillips-Andover Academy and attended Bowdoin College in Maine, but he left prior to graduation. Returning to Beverly, Ray served a medical apprenticeship to a local doctor, then enrolled at Harvard Medical School and eventually concluded his studies at the Medical School of Maine, receiving his degree in 1827 at age twenty.

From 1827 until 1841, Dr. Ray engaged in private practice in Maine while developing a specialty in mental illness. In 1838, he published a major work entitled *Treatise on the Medical Jurisprudence of Insanity*, which

Dr. Isaac Ray.

went through five editions by 1871. In that volume, Ray expressed the belief that court proceedings affecting the insane should be the special province of the medical expert witness. Only the testimony of such a trained professional, Ray maintained, could distinguish between feigned and genuine insanity. The book established Ray as an expert in this field and led to his appointment as medical superintendent at the Maine State Hospital, where he presided from 1841 to 1845. While at his Maine post, Ray, along with twelve other medical superintendents of public and private hospitals for the insane, founded an organization in 1844 that evolved into the American Psychiatric Association, making psychiatry the oldest medical specialty in the United States.

During his tenure at Maine's major mental facility, Dr. Ray accepted the directorship of Butler Hospital in Providence, then just in its planning stage. He had returned from a survey tour of European mental hospitals by December 1847, when Butler Hospital admitted its first patient. For the next two decades, until his departure for Philadelphia in 1866, Ray zealously operated the hospital in its tranquil pastoral setting on the west bank of the Seekonk River. A private facility, the hospital was an early example of the "asylum" approach to the treatment of the mentally ill and a vast improvement over the prisonlike facilities then prevalent for housing the insane. Ray knew that as an employee of private philanthropists he would be free from the political intrusions of state government.

Butler Hospital was also an outstanding example of local philanthropy. Nicholas Brown II (profiled earlier) made a then huge $30,000 donation toward the effort to establish it, only to be outdone by Providence merchant and real estate developer Cyrus Butler (1767–1849), who advanced $40,000 on the condition that $40,000 more should be contributed from other sources and that an additional $50,000 should be raised and kept as a reserve fund. These financial goals were achieved, and the state-of-the-art hospital opened in 1847; it was named in Butler's honor less than two years before his death, on August 22, 1849, at the age of eighty-two.

By 1860, the facility consisted of about 140 acres (since reduced), much of it used for farming, plus several architecturally beautiful and well-arranged buildings designed by James C. Bucklin and his apprentice Thomas Tefft, with a total capacity for 108 patients. The hospital included no facilities for laboratory or surgical work, reflecting Dr. Ray's belief that clean air, commodious quarters and comfortable surroundings were more efficacious in producing a cure. Ray was so proficient in hospital design that in 1863 the Rhode Island Medical Society appointed him to head a committee to advise the trustees of the newly created Rhode Island Hospital on the construction and arrangement of its buildings.

Ray continued to write and lecture on the professional care of the mentally ill during his period of superintendency, earning an international reputation for his insights on both the legal aspects of confinement for mental illness and the treatment of this disease, as well as gaining for Butler a reputation as an outstanding psychiatric hospital. At the outset of his tenure, he promoted a vision of universal hospital care for all those who suffered mental illness. In 1851, the Dorr Democrats heeded this vision; motivated by a humane report on the poor and insane written by reformer Thomas Hazard (profiled herein), the General Assembly made Butler Hospital the primary Rhode Island institution for care of the insane.

Legislative allowances for treatment and the establishment of a liberal and flexible commitment standard immediately gave Butler more referrals than it could accommodate. After the Know-Nothing campaign of the mid-1850s, however, xenophobia directed at Irish Catholics overcame the legislature, Butler Hospital and Ray himself. In 1857, Butler instituted a restrictive admissions policy that effectively excluded many of the foreign-born who sought asylum. By the time Ray departed in 1868, he had embraced the then current trend toward a segregated system of institutional care in which wealthy or curable patients would be the beneficiaries of treatment at upscale places like Butler, while the poor, the incurable and the immigrant would be relegated to large, impersonal and custodial public facilities. Ray's brilliance was not matched by his benevolence, so in 1870 a Rhode Island State Asylum opened at the former Howard Farm in Cranston for the custodial care of those mentally ill paupers who were deemed to be "incurable."

Ray was the quintessential professional, a prolific writer and an eloquent educator. His peers made him president of the national psychiatric association from 1855 to 1859. In 1863, while at Butler, he published a book called *Mental Hygiene* "to present some practical suggestions relative to the attainment of mental soundness and vigor," and in 1873 he published an anthology entitled *Contributions to Mental Pathology*, consisting of many previously presented papers and excerpts from annual reports that he issued as Butler's superintendent, a position from which he resigned in 1868.

Ray spent the last decade of his life in Philadelphia, where his physician son Benjamin Lincoln Ray had gone to set up a general practice of medicine. Here, Isaac remained active and enjoyed a lucrative practice as an expert psychiatric witness. It appears that he now began to see flaws in the two-tier psychiatric system he had advocated. He presented a public paper to the

Philadelphia Social Science Association in 1873 that exposed and decried the abominable conditions at the Philadelphia almshouse. On March 31, 1881, only weeks after his son Benjamin died of a stroke, Isaac also passed away silently in his sleep.

According to one historian of the psychiatric profession in America, "Isaac Ray was one of the outstanding intellects among the founders of the American Psychiatric Association, and by example, as well as by his prolific and articulate writings, did more than any other American psychiatrist of his time to advance the medical professionalization of the care of the mentally ill."

# VIII
# THE ARCHITECTS
# AND ARTISTS

The four architects profiled herein are listed in order of their births. Unlike our local entrepreneurs, lawyers, politicians and reformers, their lives are more one-dimensional and focused, and their personal lives are less known. I suspect that many were accorded less acclaim in their lifetimes than we justly bestow on them today. Nonetheless, they have given us an enduring legacy of historical ambiance and physical beauty that provides us with constant enjoyment. These profiles concentrate on their lives and their productions. A close student of historic preservation might crave a more minute analysis of architectural detail, but within the confines of these short biographies such technical analysis would be as out-of-scale as descriptions of specific surgical procedures in profiles of physicians or examinations of the legal anatomy of court cases in synopses of distinguished lawyers' careers. That cautionary statement having been made, we can proceed to reconstruct the careers of our four early nineteenth-century Hall of Fame architects, leaving the technical critique and detailed description of their works to the specialist.

## JOHN HOLDEN GREENE

John Holden Greene was born in Warwick on September 1, 1777, a member of that famous and extended Kent County clan begun by John Greene that produced Rhode Island's famous Revolutionary War general, Nathanael Greene, and its wartime governor, William Greene Jr. The middle name "Holden" indicates maternal descent from Randall Holden, who, along with

John Holden Greene designed the First Congregational Church at Benefit and Benevolent Streets in 1814. Completed in 1816, it is now a house of worship for the First Unitarian Church of Providence.

John Greene and Samuel Gorton, was among the founders of Warwick in 1642. Despite this impressive lineage, John Holden Greene's parentage and early life remain obscure and will be left to the genealogist to discover.

Apart from his birth date, the earliest published notice of Greene was his move from rural Warwick to Providence in 1794, near the age of seventeen, to begin an apprenticeship with builder Caleb Ormsbee. Again, apart from his marriage around 1800 to Elizabeth Beverly, and the fact that he built his own house at 33 Thayer Street in 1806, little is known of his career until 1809, when China merchant and financier Sullivan Dorr (the father of Thomas) commissioned Greene to design his Benefit Street home on a portion of Roger Williams's original house lot. The result was an impressive three-level structure flanked by lower wings, with both the house and its outbuildings arranged in an L-shaped plan around a paved courtyard and terraced garden. The interior of the house is notable for wall paintings executed by Italian artist Michele Felice Corné, who is also credited for popularizing tomatoes in this country by convincing Americans that they were not, as popularly thought, a poisonous fruit. The Benefit Street house was the longtime residence of Thomas Wilson Dorr, who died there on December 27, 1854.

Sullivan Dorr was an Episcopalian, which may account for Greene's next commission—St. John's Cathedral on North Main Street, just downhill from the Dorr Mansion. Constructed in 1810, this Gothic edifice was inspired by noted architect Charles Bullfinch's Federal Street Church in Boston, where William Ellery Channing (see appendix) presided. St. John's was built as a simple rectangular block with a pedimented vestibule projecting from the west end; its present transepts were added in the 1860s. The church's domed ceiling also reflected the designs of Bullfinch and Greene's mentor, Caleb Ormsbee, whose First Congregational Church (1795, now demolished) employed this feature because of its acoustical properties. According to one architect, the building "is more evocative of an English parish church than a more sophisticated city structure."

Greene's other surviving house of worship is the stately First Unitarian Church on Benefit Street at the corner of Benevolent. It replaced an Ormsbee-built Congregational church that was destroyed by fire in 1814. In designing this building, Greene employed a more classical motif. Like St. John's, the building is rectangular, with a projecting vestibule to carry a very tall steeple. Its beauty prompted the Presbyterian congregation in Savannah, Georgia, to retain Greene to design its church as a replica of the Providence structure.

Often referred to as "the carpenter-architect of Providence," Greene embraced the neoclassical style known as Federal architecture in building his homes for Providence's wealthy merchants and businessmen. Many of these houses, eighteen of which are still standing (some in altered form), are distinguished by a monitor roof, portico balustrading and an elliptical fanlight doorway. The most impressive of these residences, in addition to the Dorr Mansion, are the Truman Beckwith House (1827–28) at 42 College Street, the Greene-Dyer House (1822) at 150 Power Street, the Candace Allen House (1818–22) at 12 Benevolent Street and the Benoni Cooke House (1828) at 112 South Main Street overlooking Rhode Island's World War II Memorial. Also preserved, with substantial alteration, is the original building at the Friends School (Moses Brown), built by Greene in 1819.

Greene has been described as "the most noted architect in Providence during the first fifty years of the nineteenth century." In the Dorr Mansion and his surviving church buildings, Greene inventively combined classic and Gothic elements, giving uniqueness to these structures. During a period of extensive building in Providence, Greene was much in demand as a designer. Thus, by walking through the Benefit Street–College Hill neighborhood, one can experience an area enhanced by Greene's ingenuity and characterized by his ideas. Noted architectural historian Talbot Hamlin refers to Greene's "superb series of houses and churches…that still make the hill around Brown University one of the loveliest sections of any American city."

Unfortunately, many of his buildings are gone, such as the Dexter Asylum (1830); a group of 1820s structures near Market Square, where he built a business block; the Roger Williams Bank (1824); and the First Universalist Church (1825) at the corner of Westminster and Union Streets. Another creation, known as the Franklin House, has been incorporated into the Rhode Island School of Design buildings at the northeast corner of South Main and College Streets. His own residence at 33 Thayer Street still stands.

Greene is not considered a major American architect. He lacked professional education, and like most carpenter-architects of his era, he did not enjoy the benefit of European travel and its firsthand contact with emerging (or existing) architectural trends. He relied instead on English design books, such as those by James Gibbs and Robert Adam, and on the works of Boston's renowned Charles Bullfinch and Connecticut architect and designer Asher Benjamin. Nevertheless, his most knowledgeable critic, Frank Hurdis, provides us with this assessment: "His architectural achievements are both significant and varied. Drawing from the design sources available, he reworked basic ideas, modified and embellished decorative motifs, and combined stylistic elements in a unique and ingenious manner that can only be called his own."

This master of the carpenter's art suffered a severe economic reversal and was forced into bankruptcy by the financial Panic of 1837, a setback that greatly diminished his architectural activity. He died in Providence on September 5, 1850, at the age of seventy-three, leaving behind a son, Albert Gorton Greene (1802–1868), who was a prominent attorney and a Providence municipal court judge, as well as an accomplished poet and bibliophile who served as president of the Rhode Island Historical Society for fourteen years.

# Russell Warren

Russell Warren, called by some "Rhode Island's first professional architect," was born in Tiverton on August 5, 1783, the son of Ruth Jenckes and Gamaliel Warren, a carpenter descended from *Mayflower* passenger Richard Warren. About 1803, as he neared his majority, Russell moved across Mount Hope Bay to the prosperous port town of Bristol, where his work gained favor with the town's wealthiest merchants, James DeWolf and his brother George.

At first Warren was styled as a "carpenter-builder," and build he did, most notably large neoclassical Federal-style mansions. The two most imposing were The Mount, constructed for James DeWolf on Poppasquash Neck in 1804 (and destroyed by fire in 1904), and the still-surviving Linden Place on Hope Street in the town's center, which Warren built for George DeWolf from designs suggested by Connecticut architect Asher Benjamin's *Country Builder's Assistant*. Linden Place is set impressively back from the street. Its tall two-story Corinthian columns support its third-story portico, and its exterior features

Russell Warren.

include a Palladian window and a detailed façade. The most elegant interior feature is a four-story spiral staircase rising to a glazed dome. Today, the mansion is a town cultural center maintained by the Friends of Linden Place.

Warren built a home for himself in 1805, preserved at 86 State Street, and through his DeWolf connection he became the probable, but unverified, architect of the recently renovated 1816 Bristol County Statehouse and Courthouse, which is now also a cultural center for the town and the home of Bristol's famed Fourth of July Committee. The DeWolf connection undoubtedly accounts for Warren's periodic winter sojourns in Charleston, South Carolina, where James DeWolf conducted a brisk importing business after Rhode Island banned the slave trade in 1787. Warren is known to have designed houses in Charlestown and in the area of Savannah during his years with the DeWolfs, but he sold the properties he owned in Charleston in 1825, just prior to moving his operations to Providence.

The Providence phase of his remarkable career began auspiciously. He joined the firm of William Tallman, a builder and lumber dealer, and James C. Bucklin, a rising young architect who had apprenticed with John Holden Greene. Warren's first commission was to work with them on a downtown building that would be called The Arcade. Described by architectural historian John Hutchins Cady as "the first monumental business building" in Providence, and by glib curiosity buffs as America's oldest remaining enclosed shopping mall, it was designed by Warren and Bucklin for real estate mogul Cyrus Butler (who would later endow Butler Hospital) and the Arcade Realty Company.

The pioneering Greek Revival marketplace extended on a north–south axis from Westminster Street to Weybosset Street. The granite walls of this three-level structure were 216 feet long, with center projections giving it the form of a cross. A central corridor on the first level went street-to-street, and at each end the specific contributions of Warren and Bucklin were distinguished. The building was supported at each end by six granite columns quarried at Joseph Olney's Bare Ledge site in Johnston and hauled to Providence on sledges by teams of oxen under the supervision of lumberman and partner William Tallman. The Ionic columns were twenty-one feet high and three feet wide—and reputedly, said Cady, "the largest monoliths in America at the time of erection."

Warren was the choice of the Arcade Realty Company as the principal designer of the Westminster Street end. Bucklin did most of the design on the Weybosset Street façade. Bucklin placed a parapet above the columns in emulation of an arcade he had seen in Philadelphia. Warren chose a pediment. Warren's other major Greek Revival structure, also designed in conjunction with Bucklin, was the Westminster Congregational Church, erected on Matthewson Street in 1829.

With the monumental work on the Arcade completed in 1828, Warren proudly identified himself as "architect" in the *Providence Directory*, completing his transition from carpenter-builder. His new status altered his methods; he supervised fewer of his buildings on site, he devoted more office time to design and he began to sell his plans to carpenters or prospective homeowners.

Warren ended his association with William Tallman and James Bucklin in 1835 and partnered briefly with the renowned Alexander Jackson Davis of New York City, to whom Warren's sons, William and Osborn, were then apprenticed. This arrangement, which involved much travel, ended in 1836, but the influence of Davis on Warren's work was considerable; from Davis, Warren learned to adapt and combine architectural styles and to blend the irregularity of his picturesque Bristol homes with the geometrical details of the Greek Revival form.

Warren's final professional affiliation was with his son Osborn, with the two working as Russell Warren & Son from 1836 onward until Osborn's death in 1854. Warren's later work was performed not only in Providence and Bristol but also in the Rhode Island towns of Newport and Warren and in the flourishing southeastern communities of New Bedford and Fall River.

As one admirer of his work has noted, Warren

*is significant not only for the quality, scope, and inventiveness of his work, but for his part in the professionalization of architecture and the separation of the roles of the designer and the builder…His ingenious often fanciful adaptation of forms and uncommon sense of scale distinguish his work from other practitioners of the period.*

Warren's marriage in 1805 to Sarah Gladding produced two daughters and five sons before she died in 1817. He promptly married Lydia Gladding, his sister-in-law, in 1818, a union that gave him two more daughters. At least two of Warren's sons followed him into the field of architecture, but his son and partner Osborn predeceased him. Warren produced little surviving work of note during the final decade of his life, except for his 1856 Henry Lippitt House at 198–200 Hope Street in Providence. He died on November 16, 1860, at the age of seventy-five.

# James C. Bucklin

Records say that Providence architect James C. Bucklin was a native of Pawtucket, but in view of his family's Rehoboth origins, the place of his birth on July 26, 1801, was probably on the east side of the Blackstone, an area not acquired by Rhode Island until 1862. His parents were James and Lorania (Pearce) Bucklin. When his father died only a year and a half after his birth, James's widowed mother moved with him to Providence, where he would live for the remainder of his long life.

Bucklin received a common school education, and at age fourteen he was apprenticed to carpenter-builder John Holden Greene. After seven years of training, he entered into a business partnership with lumber dealer William Tallman, and the new firm, styled Tallman & Bucklin, became a large and prosperous architectural and building supply company. In 1828, when Bucklin was only twenty-seven, his firm joined with Russell Warren in the design and construction of the Providence Arcade (described in the Warren profile). For Bucklin's design of the Weybosset end of this classic Greek Revival structure, he looked to John Haviland's stepped parapet on the Philadelphia Arcade, which Bucklin had visited in 1826. In 1944, before historic preservation fever hit Providence, the venerable Arcade

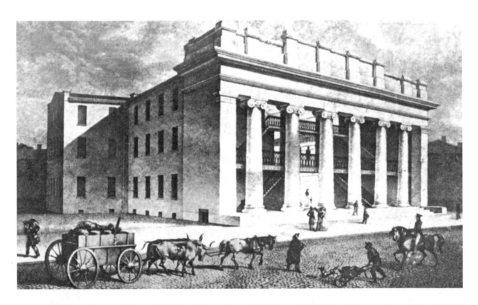

James C. Bucklin and Russell Warren were the architects of the Providence Arcade in 1828. Bucklin was reputedly the principal designer of the Weybosset Street façade (shown here).

almost fell victim to the wrecking ball, and even today it stands vacant, its fate uncertain.

In the year following their Arcade triumph, the team of Warren and Bucklin combined again, using the Greek temple motif, to design the Westminster Congregational Church on Matthewson Street. Eventually, the team dissolved when Russell Warren left Bucklin's firm in 1835.

Tallman & Bucklin gained another superb architect in 1847, when young Thomas Alexander Tefft became an employee of the company, serving as a draftsman while a student at Brown University. According to architectural historian William McKenzie Woodward, during the 1830s and '40s "Bucklin continued to provide his patrons with sober, classical houses, schools, churches, business blocks, and libraries...many finished with stucco and often scored in imitation of stone."

Still prominent among his surviving buildings are Manning Hall (1834) and Rhode Island Hall (1840) at Brown University, funded through the generosity of John Nicholas Brown II; Shakespeare Hall at 128–134 Dorrance Street; the arsenal of the Providence Marine Corps of Artillery (1839–40) on Benefit Street, now a military museum; the Rhode Island Historical Society Cabinet (1844) at 68 Waterman Street, now used for offices by Brown University; Athenaeum Row (circa 1845), a New York–style apartment building on Benefit Street across from the Licht Judicial Complex consisting of five four-story brick row houses; and the Butler Hospital Building (1847), built with the assistance of Thomas Tefft from specifications devised by Dr. Isaac Ray and Dr. Luther V. Bell in accordance with the new and innovative theories concerning treatment of the mentally disabled. Now demolished, the block-long Washington Row Building (1843–45), an impressive Greek Revival structure on the west side of Market Square, was the largest building in Providence at the time of its completion. Built for the Providence-Washington Insurance Company during the presidency of Sullivan Dorr, it housed the Providence Journal Company from 1844 to 1871 and a telegraph office when that invention came to Providence in 1847.

Thomas Tefft's brief association with Tallman & Bucklin from 1847 to 1851 apparently influenced Bucklin's later efforts. When the partnership ended in the mid-1850s, Bucklin continued his impressive output for another two decades. Notable survivors from this period are the Hiram Hill House (1864) on Charlesfield Street, the Hay Block on Dorrance Street (1867) and the Monohasset Mill (1868) on Kinsley Street (a building once owned by the author). The demolished creations include the third Howard Hall Building (1859) on Dorrance Street, the Hoppin Homestead Building (1875) on Westminster Street, the Providence Music Hall on Westminster Street and the Thomas and Paulina Wright Davis Mansion (1869), a Gothic villa on Chalkstone Avenue that was demolished to make way for the Veterans' Administration Hospital.

According to a 1908 genealogical profile, Bucklin was "the architect of some 300 mill structures and many fine residences as well as business buildings in various parts of the country." In 1867–68, he built additions to the Old Statehouse at 150 Benefit Street and made alterations to the Providence Athenaeum. He even designed numerous memorials in Swan Point Cemetery for leading Rhode Island families.

While Bucklin's business life was busy, his civic involvement was more limited. As a young man, he was active in the Rhode Island militia, holding the rank of first lieutenant in the First Light Infantry, and later in life he was a charter member of the Squantum Club when this gentlemen's dining association opened in 1871. Bucklin was known as "a great reader of good books" who "was fond of his home and family." That family included his wife, the former Lucy Dailey, daughter of ship captain Daniel Dailey of Providence, whom he married on March 16, 1829. The couple had five children and lived a long life together. Lucy died in November 1888 after fifty-nine years of marriage; James died in September 1890, at the age of eighty-eight.

## Thomas Alexander Tefft

In 1856, the year that thirty-year-old Thomas Alexander Tefft embarked on an educational and architectural tour of Europe—from which he would not return alive—Massachusetts bard John Greenleaf Whittier published his famous poem "Maud Muller," containing these memorable lines: "For of all sad words of tongue or pen, the saddest are these: 'It might have been!'" In some sense, Whittier wrote Tefft's epitaph. Thomas Alexander Tefft was a very important Rhode Island architect, despite his youthfulness and very brief career. Had he lived long, say the critics, he would have been a major American architect.

Tefft was born on August 3, 1826, in Richmond, Rhode Island, a very rural Rhode Island town, then and now. The names of his parents are unknown, and the public records shed no light on his early education, yet he is probably the town of Richmond's most famous native son.

Young Thomas was brilliant and had a talent for drawing. These attributes were discovered by school agent Henry Barnard when he was

Thomas Alexander Tefft.

conducting his statewide survey of public education in 1843 and 1844. Acting on Barnard's advice, Tefft moved to Providence in 1845 and enrolled at Brown University (probably with Barnard's sponsorship) in 1847. During his four collegiate years, he worked as a draftsman for Tallman & Bucklin. He might have selected this architectural firm because it was the largest in the city, but as Barnard's protégé he probably selected it because of the recent work the company had done in constructing ten primary schools, six grammar schools and the first Providence high school (1843) in accordance with plans set in motion in 1840–41 by school committee chairman Thomas Wilson Dorr.

Tefft made his mark immediately. While only a twenty-one-year-old freshman at Brown, he designed (with James Bucklin's guidance) one of the architectural marvels of mid-nineteenth-century Providence: the Union Passenger Depot of the Providence-Worcester Railroad Company. At the time of its completion in 1848, on filled land once part of Providence's saltwater cove, it was the largest train station in the country, spanning 625 feet in length. As late as 1885, this Romanesque structure was selected in an architectural survey as one of the twenty best-designed buildings in the United States. This massive building (destroyed by fire in 1896) embodied the two principal architectural interests that occupied Tefft until his untimely death: the introduction of ornamental brick architecture to the United States and the employment of a building style based on the tenth- and eleventh-century round-arched Romanesque architecture of Italy and Germany, a form of construction then being revived in Berlin and Munich.

While still in college, Tefft also designed such significant surviving structures as Lawrence Hall at Williams College in Massachusetts, containing

America's first central library plan, and the Cannelon Cotton Mill in Indiana (1849), which strongly resembles several unattributed Rhode Island mills that display similar flexible massing, brick construction and the decorative style of Lombard Romanesque architecture.

After graduation in 1851, Tefft set out on his own, acquiring a large architectural library and preparing several hundred drawings and building designs for existing commissions or prospective use (now on deposit at Brown's John Hay Library and the Rhode Island Historical Society). Those commissions included public schools (the Barnard connection), railroad stations (inspired by his Providence masterpiece), large fireproof mills (in accordance with insurance standards pioneered by Zachariah Allen), large commercial buildings, churches and banks. His main source of steady income, however, was the design of elaborate College Hill and Newport residences with carriage houses, built of brownstone and red brick with an Italianate or Renaissance Revival motif.

Among Tefft's surviving works from the early 1850s are the original Central Congregational Church at 226 Benefit Street (1853–56), now part of the Rhode Island School of Design complex; the Tully Bowen House (1853) at 389 Benefit Street; the Robert Lippitt House (1854) at 193 Hope Street; and several other East Side homes.

Not content with the stunning success he had achieved in his four years with Tallman & Bucklin and his six years of private practice, Tefft set out for Europe in December 1856 to study Romanesque architecture firsthand, to learn European methods of architectural education and to meet with noted European architects. While on his grand tour, he became interested in the application of the decimal theory to a gold-based currency to be made universal, and he read his paper on this topic before the British Association for the Promotion of Social Science. He also engaged in other intellectual activities during his travels, including the publication of a series of articles on architecture for *The Canyon*, a professional journal. Several of his letters on European social and political affairs were printed in the *New York Times*.

In addition to England, Tefft visited France, Switzerland, Germany and Italy, home of Lombard Romanesque architecture. On his second visit to Florence, he was stricken with a fever and died on December 12, 1859, three years into his travels, at the age of thirty-three. His death occurred at the home of his friend, American neoclassical sculptor Hiram Powers. Tefft's remains were interred temporarily in the English Cemetery in Florence but were eventually brought back to his native Rhode Island.

It was Thomas Tefft's goal to return to American brimming with information and ideas regarding the teaching and practice of architecture. He returned in a coffin. One can only speculate on what Tefft's lofty achievements and legacy might have been had he survived his European journey.

# JAMES SULLIVAN LINCOLN

James Sullivan Lincoln was Rhode Island's premier portrait painter of the mid-nineteenth century and was acclaimed by his peers as the "Father of Rhode Island Art." Unlike Rhode Island's famed Gilbert Stuart, who was nationally recognized as the portraitist of the American founders (see appendix), Lincoln painted mainly Rhode Island places and personalities, including many of the "makers" profiled herein.

Lincoln was born on a farm in Taunton, Massachusetts, on May 13, 1811, the oldest of the six children of Sullivan and Keziah Lincoln. (Taunton was distinctive in that it had been founded in 1639 by Elizabeth Poole a year after another woman, Anne Hutchinson, established the Rhode Island town of Portsmouth with her followers.) James was orphaned while still in his teens, but he soon traveled eighteen miles westward to cosmopolitan Providence, where he first became an apprentice to the engraving firm of Horton & Hidden and then to Providence portraitist C.T. Hinckley. While working with Hinckley, Lincoln discovered his talent for painting, especially portraiture, and in 1832 he began a sixty-year career during which he produced over four thousand painted and photographic images. His oils, crayons and photographs were the media he used to create and preserve the faces of nineteenth-century Rhode Islanders, recording his progress from 1837 to 1887

James Sullivan Lincoln.

in a handwritten logbook of his commissions, now preserved at the Rhode Island Historical Society Library.

Lincoln received numerous commissions to depict local men, women and families during the course of six decades, and he did so by rendering faithful likenesses guided by his creative instincts. It has been said that his calm and objective temperament allowed him to paint both those he admired and those he did not. Not only did this attitude comport with his temperament, but it also enabled him to paint politically incompatible clients. Lincoln's contemporary subjects included such Rhode Island Hall of Fame inductees as Samuel Slater, Zachariah Allen, John Howland, William Read Staples, Henry Barnard, Wilkins Updike, Elisha Dyer II, Ambrose Burnside, William Sprague II, Amos Chafee Barstow and John Russell Bartlett. His portraits of fourteen Rhode Island governors adorn the walls of the statehouse. In addition, Lincoln painted copies of such earlier Rhode Island notables as the Reverend James Manning (1738–1791), the first president of Brown University, and General William Barton (1748–1831), a Revolutionary War hero.

Amazingly, the man who revealed and preserved on his canvasses the faces of so many Rhode Island leaders of his era is not well remembered himself. None of the standard biographical volumes containing entries detailing the lives of nineteenth-century Rhode Islanders includes a profile of Lincoln. Had he not signed his canvasses, he would have remained almost anonymous, despite the lofty title conferred on him posthumously.

Lincoln was not known to be active outside the field of art, but at the end of his long career he joined with four younger artists—Edward Bannister, Charles Walter Stetson, George W. Whitaker and Sydney Richmond Burleigh (all Hall of Famers)—to form the Providence Art Club in 1881, with Lincoln as its first president.

This quiet family man, praised by contemporaries for his "gentle and loving nature," possessed a modesty that belied his stature as the premier portraitist of Rhode Islanders. He lived in various modest Providence dwellings with his wife, Rosina (whom he married in 1844), and their daughter, Ellen, the subject of one of his most admired portraits. Lincoln died in Providence on January 19, 1888. A year after his death, the Providence Art Club commissioned a bust of Lincoln by visiting Italian sculptor Appolonj that still graces the organization Lincoln helped to create. Among those profiled herein, Lincoln is unique in that his brief biography is illustrated by his self-portrait, the original of which is on display at the Providence Art Club.

# IX

# THE LITERATI

## CATHARINE R. (ARNOLD) WILLIAMS

In early nineteenth-century Rhode Island, a woman's role was sharply circumscribed by tradition. A woman—even one of high social station—was thought of mainly as a wife and a mother. Those who ventured beyond the home (religious nuns excepted) might find work from the 1830s onward as a teacher in a primary school, as a school committee member (after 1843) or as a midwife—all child-related duties. Those who were bolder could express themselves by writing or as social reformers. The latter became involved in the excitement and challenge of the first great age of American reform, a variegated movement that swept the country in the three decades prior to the Civil War.

Catharine R. (Arnold) Williams chose both writing and reform as the outlets for her creative and social impulses. She was born in Providence on December 31, 1787, the daughter of Amey Read and sea captain Alfred Arnold, who was descended from an old-line Rhode Island family. Her mother died when Catharine was very young, so her father entrusted her upbringing to two of her maiden aunts, "ladies of the old school," who gave her, said Catharine, a comfortable and very religious upbringing. She did not leave the shelter of their home until she was twenty-three, after the death of one aunt and the marriage of the other, and later commented on her difficulty in coping with "the real world."

Shortly after leaving her aunts' home, she found herself in a troubled marriage. In 1824, she became the bride of Rhode Islander Horatio N. Williams and moved to western New York State, where she had his daughter,

Catharine R. (Arnold) Williams.

then returned to Providence in 1826 and divorced him. She later remarked that the cleric who performed the wedding service had just presided at a funeral and did not remove his mourning vestments, an omen, she stated, that foreshadowed the result of her marriage. Henceforth, she carried his surname and bad memories of this experience. She never remarried, but once established in her writing career, she adopted a son.

Catharine Williams's first publication, *Original Poems, on Various Subjects*, some of whose verses were composed in her teens, met with a favorable local reception. It was followed in 1829 by *Religion at Home*, a story undoubtedly based on her own upbringing. Her first important work was her fifth book, *Fall River: An Authentic Record* (1833), an exposé that dealt, in the manner of an investigative reporter, with the sensational murder trial of the Reverend Ephraim K. Avery, Bristol's newly installed Methodist minister, for the brutal December 1832 murder of promiscuous, pregnant millworker Sarah Cornell in the Fall River section of the town of Tiverton. Avery was acquitted in a trial that Williams and most others considered to be a miscarriage of justice, one that showed partiality for males over females and the influence of social standing over those who lacked it.

In 1839, she produced a still useful volume on Rhode Island history entitled *Biography of Revolutionary Heroes*. It contained interesting sketches of the lives of General William Barton (captor of British general Richard Prescott) and Captain Stephen Olney (who rendered distinguished service throughout the war, especially at Yorktown).

According to Williams, her best book was a historical novel entitled *The Neutral French; or the Exiles of Nova Scotia* (1841), a subject that she spent time in Canada researching. It told with great sympathy the tragic story of the British displacement of the Acadian French in the 1750s during the final phase of the Great War for Empire. With some justification, she believed that her novel served as the inspiration for Henry Wadsworth Longfellow's epic work *Evangeline: A Tale of Acadie*, published in 1847.

Williams did not confine herself to writing. She publicly advocated for improvements in the status of women and in the condition of workers. As a sea captain's daughter, she opposed the naval practice of flogging, and she also decried the use of capital punishment in the aftermath of John Gordon's execution. She was a staunch supporter of the reform wing of the Democratic Party, and in her popular two-volume work *Annals of the Aristocracy...of Rhode Island* (1843–45), she criticized the elitism and conservatism of Rhode Island's upper class.

During the Dorr Rebellion and its aftermath, Williams became an ally and confidante of Dorr and corresponded with him. As historian Ronald Formisano has shown, this constitutional controversy and Dorr's imprisonment led to the active involvement of women in Rhode Island politics for the first time. The Dorr Rebellion served as their political coming-out party. Both Williams and Frances (Whipple) Green McDougall vigorously and successfully campaigned for Dorr's liberation from prison. Williams organized a women's group for that goal, and she assisted McDougall in writing *Might and Right*, a cogent defense of Dorr and the People's Constitution.

In 1845, the year of Dorr's release from prison, she concluded her publishing career, which had included twelve works of history, fiction, verse and social criticism. In 1849, she traveled to Brooklyn to take care of the ailing aunt who raised her. When her aunt died three years later, she returned to Rhode Island and took up residence with her daughter, Amey, in Johnston. Thereafter, she worked on her autobiography, traveled occasionally, returned to her former home in Providence at the corner of

Olney and North Main Streets and led a relatively uneventful life until her death in Providence on October 11, 1872, at the age of eighty-four.

During her retirement, Williams enjoyed the distinction of being elected an honorary member of several local learned societies, a recognition not conferred, she once remarked, on females in Rhode Island. She furnished her unpublished autobiography to prolific historian Sidney S. Rider, who later used it in writing his *Biographical Memoirs of Three Rhode Island Authors* (1880). In a note appended to her autobiography, Rider described this "remarkable person" as follows:

> *Rather short in stature and quite stout, very slovenly in dress, her bonnet always on one side of her head—wears no hoops—and most always a dirty dress—her small eyes twinkle between two lightish brown curls on either side of her head—and with her squeaking voice you have a complete picture of Mrs. Williams—she is an inveterate Talker and is always ready to talk to any one as long as they will listen—she is deeply interested in politics.*

Despite her financially comfortable status, gained by inheritance and publishing, Catharine Williams believed that the female writer's task was not only to uplift and enlighten but also to relieve social distress—"to comfort the afflicted, succor the persecuted, strengthen the weak, and raise up those who are fallen." She performed her task well.

## FRANCES HARRIET (WHIPPLE) GREEN McDOUGALL

"A Rhode Island Original" is a description used by Sarah O'Dowd to title her biography of Frances Whipple. It aptly describes one of Rhode Island's most significant mid-nineteenth-century writers and reformers.

Frances was born in Smithfield in September 1805, the eldest of the four children of George Washington Whipple and Ann Scott, both of whom were members of old and extended Rhode Island families. The Whipple clan was prominent in Smithfield, but according to sketchy accounts George "was reduced to poverty" around 1817, when Frances was twelve, and "the little blue-eyed Fanny was left to support herself by her own industry, and to depend on such means of improvement as the common school."

By the time she was twenty-three, Frances had moved to Providence to attend a private school taught by Dr. Peter W. Ferris, with whom she

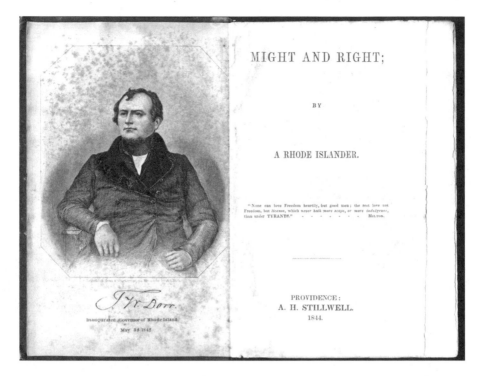

MIGHT AND RIGHT;

BY

A RHODE ISLANDER.

"None can love Freedom heartily, but good men; the rest love not Freedom, but *license*, which *never hath more scope, or more indulgence*, than under TYRANTS." - - - - - - Milton.

PROVIDENCE:
A. H. STILLWELL.
1844.

Inaugurated Governor of Rhode Island
May 3-4-1842

Frances Harriet (Whipple) Green McDougall was the principal author of *Might and Right*, the most detailed defense of the Dorr Rebellion. Her biographer and others have been unable to find her likeness in local repositories, but one may eventually be located in California, where she spent the final seventeen years of her eventful life.

interacted intellectually for the remainder of her time in Rhode Island. In May 1829, the year after enrolling at the Ferris school, she began to edit and publish her first periodical; named the *Original*, it expired in 1830 after two issues despite her ambitious plans. This pioneering periodical was notable for its historical sketch of Central Falls, then known as "Chocolate Mills" because a chocolate factory was located there, and for "Peggy O'Morven," an empathetic story of the hardships endured by Irish immigrants then coming to Rhode Island. The second and final issue gave evidence of Frances Whipple's emerging antislavery sympathies by containing the poem "Autumn Thoughts," contributed by twenty-two-year-old abolitionist poet John Greenleaf Whittier, "the bard of freedom."

By the late 1830s, the reformist spirit of America's "Age of Equalitarianism" turned Whipple's interest increasingly toward some of the causes of that period, especially temperance, abolition and workers' rights. In 1838, she published *The Memoirs of Elleanor Eldridge*, a defense of a local free black and

Indian woman who successfully sought the recovery of her seized property. Then Whipple wrote a novel entitled *The Mechanic* (1841), urging respect for workers, and during 1842, she edited the *Wampanoag and Operatives' Journal*, a periodical designed to improve the condition of female factory hands in Fall River (which then was partly in Rhode Island).

In these years, she was the most prolific antislavery writer in Providence, contributing to William Lloyd Garrison's *Liberator* and other periodicals and editing two collections of antislavery essays, *The Envoy* (1840) and *Liberty Chimes* (1845). According to O'Dowd, Whipple's interests intersected with those of her Smithfield neighbors Arnold Buffum, who owned a Fall River mill, and his daughter, Elizabeth Buffum Chace. The Buffums (profiled herein) were also militant opponents of slavery and contributed writings on that subject and on spiritualism to Whipple's publications.

Whipple also held Rhode Island's Native Americans in high regard. In 1840, she wrote her longest and best poem concerning the March 26, 1676, battle at Central Falls between Narragansett sachem Canonchet (Nanuntenoo) and Captain Michael Pierce of the Plymouth Colony, which resulted in a decisive victory for Canonchet in revenge for the Great Swamp Massacre of Narragansetts in December 1675.

From a Rhode Island perspective, Whipple's *Might and Right* is her most important work. In this book, written with assistance from Catharine Williams, she persuasively defended the Dorr Rebellion with logic and fervor. Her support of Dorr's efforts contrasted markedly with the position of her first cousin John Whipple, the attorney who teamed with Daniel Webster before the U.S. Supreme Court to repudiate Dorr's movement for constitutional change.

Published in 1844, shortly after her first marriage, *Might and Right* contained a sketch of Dorr's life, and it was defiantly dedicated "to Thomas Wilson Dorr, the true and tried patriot, the Fearless Defender of Human Rights," as Dorr sat in prison under a life sentence for treason against the state. According to the recollections of historian Sidney Rider, she was "a very violent partisan of Mr. Dorr. Unfortunately for her personal comfort, she was ever on the unpopular side of every question in Rhode Island."

Perhaps her "unpopular" views influenced her decision to leave the repressive political atmosphere of Rhode Island for more progressive locations. Also disruptive and discouraging was her brief marriage in Springfield, Massachusetts, to artist Charles C. Green. Like her colleague Catharine Williams, she soon filed for divorce, which was granted on September 20, 1847, for the familiar grounds of desertion and abandonment, as well as for the more unusual claim of "extreme cruelty and gross misbehavior." After this breakup, she went to her sister Mary Congdon's home in Pomfret, Connecticut, and then boarded for a time in Bridgeport with the family of the Reverend Samuel Brittan, a noted author, medium and spiritualist.

Her contacts with Rhode Island now severed, Frances Green moved on to New York City and other parts unknown, turning her attention to the writing of works on slavery and spiritualism and a textbook on botany. Then, in 1861, this talented and restless woman ventured to California, where she met and married her second husband, William C. McDougall, a miner, a former California assemblyman and the brother of the state's second governor, John McDougall. In her new home, Frances McDougall lent her pen to the cause of women's rights and assumed the role of a medium, speaking and writing messages dictated to her from the spirit world. She died in Oakland, California, on June 10, 1878.

# SARAH HELEN (POWER) WHITMAN

The third member of Rhode Island's early nineteenth-century group of famous literary women was Sarah Helen (Power) Whitman. She was born in Providence on January 19, 1803, the daughter of the former Anna Marsh and Providence merchant and sea captain Nicholas Power. Helen's father (she preferred to be called Helen) was a descendant of the Nicholas Power who had arrived in Providence from Ireland during the 1640s. His progeny included Hope Power, the mother of the famed Brown brothers of Providence. John Brown built his splendid mansion in 1786 on Power Street, just south of Helen's home (the mansion is now a house museum owned by the Rhode Island Historical Society). Helen's father was not as fortunate financially as some other members of the clan but was ruined by the commercial restrictions imposed on American commerce prior to the War of 1812. He was captured at sea by the British after the outbreak of war, and when he was released in 1815, he continued his maritime ventures and did not return to Providence until the early 1830s. Perhaps this abandonment is why Helen seldom used her maiden name.

Deprived of the financial and moral support of her father at the age of ten, Helen was sent to live with an aunt in Jamaica, Long Island, and attended a Quaker school there. Upon her return to Providence in her teens, she enrolled at a private school, where she learned to read French, German and Italian and began to develop her skills as a poetess.

Sarah Helen (Power)
Whitman.

On one of her trips to partake of the rich cultural atmosphere of Boston, she met John Winslow Whitman, a well-to-do and highly literate Boston lawyer, whom she wed in 1828, when she was twenty-five. John Whitman, more a writer than an attorney, was the publisher of two periodicals, the *Batchelors' Journal* and the *Boston Spectator and Ladies' Album*, to which Helen contributed some poetry.

Unlike the marriages of Catharine Williams and Frances Whipple, the Whitmans had a compatible and presumably happy relationship, but unfortunately it was also short. John Whitman died in 1833, leaving Helen a young widow. She returned to Providence shortly thereafter to live with her mother in the family home at 88 Benefit Street, and she never remarried. By that time, her father had returned from his travels, although the details of his daughter's reaction to this belated arrival are unknown.

During her stay in Boston, she had become acquainted with many of that vibrant city's cultural leaders, and her heritage as a Power and the force of her own talent and intellect also allowed her to move among Providence's cultural elite. From the time of her first published poem in 1829, she steadily placed her verses in various women's magazines and wrote scholarly articles on modern European literature. She also published critical essays in praise of Goethe, Shelley, Coleridge and American author Ralph Waldo Emerson, whom she came to know.

From the mid-1830s and for more than forty years thereafter, Helen maintained Rhode Island's foremost literary salon at her home. It was frequented by many prominent non–Rhode Island writers and intellectuals, including Emerson, Bronson Alcott, Sarah Hale, Margaret Fuller, John Hay (when Lincoln's famous private secretary and biographer was a student at Brown) and, most legendary of all, Edgar Allan Poe.

Much time and attention (perhaps too much) has been devoted to the brief but intense romantic relationship between Helen Whitman and America's master of the macabre. Her first glimpse of Poe came in 1845 as he strolled along Benefit Street, but they did not meet until 1848, a year after Poe's wife died. As an ardent admirer of Poe's work, in February 1848 Whitman addressed an unsigned poetic valentine to him that was subsequently published in the *New York Home Journal*. This gesture naturally sparked Poe's interest, and learning Whitman's identity, he sent her an unsigned poem, which is now known as "To Helen." The two platonic lovers met in Providence in September 1848. Poe proposed marriage, but she rejected the offer primarily because of Poe's excessive drinking and the disapproval of her domineering mother, who knew that Poe was a womanizer as well as an alcoholic. This whirlwind on-and-off relationship ended on December 23, 1848, when a dejected Poe left Providence, never to see Helen again. He erratically pursued several other women prior to his death on October 7, 1849, at the age of forty after an orgy of drinking. In 1860, Whitman published a defense of her former suitor's work entitled *Edgar Poe and His Critics*.

After her dalliance with Poe, Whitman began to compose articles on spiritualism, the first of which appeared in 1851 in the *New York Tribune*. She published her first collection of verse, entitled *Hours of Life, and Other Poems*, in 1853. Although she advocated women's rights, individual development and perfectibility and educational reform, the genteel Helen Whitman, unlike Catharine Williams or Frances Whipple, did not expound on the currently explosive topics of abolitionism or Rhode Island political reform.

Whitman continued to write her poetry and conduct her salons into her seventies, and as she grew older, she became increasingly interested in mysticism and the occult. She died childless in Providence on June 27, 1878, aged seventy-five, and was laid to rest in Providence's North Burial Ground.

The bulk of her estate was used to publish another volume containing her poetry and that of her sister. Though she had not espoused the cause of abolitionism, she left a substantial sum to the Providence Association for the Benefit of Colored Children.

With Catharine Williams and Frances Whipple, Sarah Helen (Power) Whitman was one of a trio of contemporaneous women writers that has never been replicated in Rhode Island.

## WILKINS UPDIKE

Wilkins Updike, a member of the noted Updike family of North Kingstown, was the youngest of eleven children of Lodowick and Abigail Updike, and he himself became the father of twelve. He was born on January 8, 1784, to a paternal line originating in Prussia and including Richard Smith, the first white settler in the Narragansett Country. Wilkins's mother was a member of the prosperous Gardiner family of Narragansett.

Wilkins Updike.

Wilkins was raised near Wickford at Cocumscussoc, also known as Smith's Castle, and studied with tutors prior to attending a prestigious private academy in Plainfield, Connecticut. Rather than move on to college, he studied law, first in the office of James Lanman of Norwich, Connecticut, who later became a U.S. senator; then under Newport Federalist leaders William Hunter and Asher Robbins, the latter of whom also became a U.S. senator; and finally under Federalist congressman Elisha R. Potter Sr. in Little Rest (now Kingston), where he would eventually make his home. Updike was admitted to the Rhode Island bar in 1807.

As a lawyer, Wilkins Updike was quite successful. He became known both for his wit and his eloquence. One associate described him as a "very effective debater, his logic being very convincing." He drew his clientele mainly from Washington and Kent Counties.

On September 23, 1809, the young attorney married a woman, Abigail Watson, from a prominent South County family, who would bear his twelve children prior to her death in 1843. The couple was living contentedly at Cocumscussoc in 1812 when financial disaster overtook Updike. One of his brothers (who has remained unidentified) went into business in New York and failed, and Wilkins was the guarantor of his brother's business loan. To satisfy the deficiency judgment against him, Wilkins was forced to sell the Updikes' historic 1678 homestead and three hundred acres of land to Benjamin Congdon of Warwick on December 31, 1812.

Cocumscussoc was not just another house. As a center of South County intellectual and social life, this rural estate just north of Wickford was the subject of a fascinating 1971 book by agricultural historian and former URI president Carl R. Woodward, who entitled it *Plantation in Yankeeland*. The loss of Cocumscussoc—or Smith's Castle, as it was also called— greatly affected Wilkins Updike and left him heartbroken. Never again could he be induced to pass within sight of the old family mansion or even refer to it in conversation.

Fortunately, Updike proved resilient. He and his family made a new home in the South Kingstown village of Little Rest, the domain of the Elisha Potters. Little Rest, where the county courthouse and statehouse was within walking distance from his home, was an ideal place for the aspiring attorney. Combining law and politics, Updike represented South Kingstown in the General Assembly for many terms.

Updike's most notable political achievement was his leadership role in bringing Henry Barnard to Rhode Island in 1843 to reform and modernize the state's educational system. His other important legislative initiatives included the enactment of a law to give married women the right to own property in their own names and a successful campaign in the early 1850s to repudiate Rhode Island's Revolutionary War debt because, in his opinion, it had been acquired by Providence speculators with no ties to the Revolution.

Updike served as a delegate from South Kingstown in three constitutional conventions: the first state constitutional convention in 1824, the Freeman's convention in 1841–42 and the Law and Order convention in 1842, a conclave that drafted the state's first popularly written constitution. In all of these conventions, he was a stout and zealous defender of the agricultural interests and the voice of political conservatism. He also served as a Van Buren delegate to the 1836 national Democratic convention in Baltimore.

During the 1830s, the party of Andrew Jackson in Rhode Island was rural-based and very resistant to political reform. Updike and many others from South County feared that their rural ways would be overwhelmed by the Irish and other factory workers in Providence and the mills of the Blackstone Valley. The provision in the Law and Order Constitution of 1843 that each town, regardless of population, have one vote (and one vote only) in the state senate was a product of that fear. In effect, that apportionment rule gave the rural towns a veto over state legislation.

In addition to his long tenure as state representative, Updike sought higher office in 1847, when he ran for Congress in Rhode Island's Western District as a Whig. In the initial balloting, he outpolled his four rivals, but he failed to gain the required majority. In the runoff balloting four months later, he lost to Democrat Benjamin Thurston.

As his grandson Daniel Berkeley Updike perceptively observed of Wilkins, "By profession he was a lawyer. By long custom he was a legislator. But if you had essayed to go down to the heart of the real man you would have found that he was at the bottom of his nature an antiquarian." Thus, he is included herein among the writers, despite his impressive public service.

As a historian, Updike's most notable works are *Memoirs of the Rhode Island Bar* (1842), a detailed account of the development of the legal profession in Rhode Island; *The History of the Alleged State Debt* (1846), a learned but brief economic treatise on Rhode Island's Revolutionary War debt, calling for its repudiation; and his magnum opus, the *History of the Episcopal Church in Narragansett* (1847). This latter work was far more than a mere history of St. Paul's Parish in Wickford; it has been described as "a volume alone in its class, at once a foundation for the history of the Church in this commonwealth and a picture of early social life." According to Professor Woodward, "None but an ardent man of letters could have produced a work of this caliber." Today, it retains its full value as a source of information about life and society in the colonial Narragansett Country because of the prodigious original research on which it is based. In 1907, it was reprinted, together with a very personal biographical "sketch of the life of Wilkins Updike," in a large, illustrated, three-volume edition by Wilkins's illustrious grandson Daniel Berkeley Updike, the proprietor of the Merrymount Press.

For the last two decades of his long life, Wilkins Updike lived a vibrant social and intellectual existence. His Kingston home welcomed an array of prominent politicians and literati, many of whom are profiled in this book. He was especially close to Elisha R. Potter Jr., his longtime legislative colleague from South Kingstown, who succeeded Henry Barnard as state commissioner of education. In 1858, this duo commissioned James Sullivan Lincoln to paint a portrait of Barnard, which they then presented to the Rhode Island Historical Society.

Described as "a king of hospitality" at his sociointellectual gatherings, Updike made a romantic pitch to Sarah Helen Whitman, one of the regular attendees. This widowed father of twelve, then sixty-three, was politely rebuffed by the forty-four-year-old poet, who was smitten with Edgar Allan Poe.

Updike, the scholar and bibliophile, was elected to membership in many learned societies, and he had planned one more major historical work before his health declined in the early 1860s. His older brother Daniel, who had been elected the secretary of the March 1790 ratifying convention that met in the Little Rest Statehouse but adjourned without approving the federal Constitution, kept his notes on the convention until his death in 1842, when they were entrusted to the care of Wilkins. It was the latter's intention to write a chronicle of this transitional era of Rhode Island history, but such a book was never produced. In 1863, Wilkins gave this historical treasure to Secretary of State John Russell Bartlett, who then shared it with Justice William R. Staples. The judge used these notes in compiling his very useful book, *Rhode Island in the Continental Congress* (1870).

Wilkins Updike finally succumbed to a chronic illness on January 14, 1867, at the age of eighty-three. He was initially interred at Boston Neck in what is present-day Narragansett, but subsequently his remains were transferred to St. Paul's churchyard in Wickford on land donated to the church by his great-grandfather. In a testimony to the Updikes' good genes, the average age at death of his ten siblings exceeded eighty years. One of his daughters, Isabella, married Richard Kidder Randolph, the Law and Order Speaker of the House during the Dorr Rebellion and the nephew of President William

Henry Harrison. Wilkins's son Caesar Augustus was also Rhode Island's Speaker of the House from 1860 to 1862 and the father of noted book designer and printer Daniel Berkeley Updike (1860–1941).

Wilkins Updike was eulogized by his associates and successors in the state legislature, who knew him best, as "this old-fashioned gentleman, this vigorous and honest legislator, this hospitable and warm-hearted citizen, almost the last of a generation of true Rhode Island men."

## SECRETARY OF STATE JOHN RUSSELL BARTLETT

The Rhode Island Heritage Hall of Fame has developed a tradition of listing its inductees by the title of their highest public office or by the title "Dr." if they have earned that distinction in their chosen field of endeavor. John Russell Bartlett's title, though prestigious, only begins to embrace his many notable achievements. Clearly, Bartlett was Rhode Island's greatest secretary

Secretary of State
John Russell Bartlett.

of state and the one who most expanded and fulfilled the historical duties of that office, but there is more to his career than the holding of a mainly ministerial political post.

Bartlett was born in Providence on October 23, 1805, the second of the six children of Smith and Nancy (Russell) Bartlett. Shortly after his birth, his parents took the family to the Canadian town of Kingston, at the eastern end of Lake Ontario, where Smith Bartlett established a thriving mercantile business and where this American family weathered the War of 1812. One of the five American diplomats who negotiated the Treaty of Ghent that ended the conflict was Providence-born Jonathan Russell (see appendix), Nancy's cousin.

Bartlett was raised in Kingston, where he received his early education prior to studying for two years at Lowville Academy in upstate New York and then receiving a year of private tutoring in Montreal. In 1824, when he was eighteen, he returned to Providence and worked for several years as a clerk in his uncle's dry goods store on Westminster Street opposite from where the Arcade was being built by developer Cyrus Butler. When Bartlett's uncle moved his shop to the Arcade, Butler became acquainted with young John and offered him the position of clerk in Butler's Bank of North America, also located in the Arcade. By 1831, Bartlett had persuaded Butler to open a library and reading room on the building's second floor, a facility that soon evolved into the prestigious Providence Athenaeum, which Bartlett not only helped to found but also supported throughout his life.

During his twelve-year association with Rhode Island from 1824 to 1836, Bartlett left the employ of Butler to become a cashier at the Globe Bank, owned by the William Sprague family. In 1831, the year he assumed his new post, he married Eliza A. Rhodes of Pawtuxet, by whom he had seven children prior to her death on November 11, 1853. Until 1836, the couple lived in an apartment above the bank.

Bartlett embarked on a much more exciting career than that of store clerk or bank cashier when he began to paint and draw during his early years in Providence. Around 1835, he produced his most famous local image, *The Great Gale of September 1815*, an oil painting depicting the raging waters of the Providence River inundating Market Square. In addition, his association with the Athenaeum, the Franklin Society and the Rhode Island Historical Society put him in contact with the young bibliophile John Carter Brown and launched Bartlett into the world of books.

In 1836, Bartlett took a more lucrative bank position in New York City, but the bank dissolved in the Panic of 1837. In the late 1830s, he was active in the revival of the nearly defunct New-York Historical Society, and in 1843 he entered the book business with Charles Welford. This duo marketed large consignments from prominent London bookseller William C. Hall and books from their own searches. Bartlett later claimed that his firm was "the first to keep a large stock of choice old books in every department of literature, hence our establishment was the resort of literary men not only from New York, but from all parts of the country." Prominent among his regular clientele were Albert Gallatin and James Fenimore Cooper. Not content merely with selling books, however, Bartlett began to write. With Gallatin, former secretary of the treasury under Jefferson and Madison, Bartlett was prominent in the formation of the American Ethnological Society, an organization created to further the study of primitive cultures. He contributed to this scholarly endeavor as the society's corresponding secretary by publishing a book entitled *Progress of Ethnology* in 1847. He followed this work a year later with his most commercially successful volume, the still valuable *Dictionary of Americanisms: A Glossary of Words and Phrases Usually Regarded as Peculiar to the United States* (1848, rev. ed. 1857), which was later translated into Dutch and German.

In 1850, Bartlett sought other work for health and financial reasons. His political and scholarly connections brought him an appointment as the American commissioner of the Mexican Boundary Survey, a task necessitated by the American acquisition of a huge area from Mexico in its Treaty of Guadalupe-Hidalgo ending the Mexican War. This post afforded Bartlett an opportunity to combine ethnological and scientific exploration with his artistic skill. During his two-and-a-half-year tenure in the United States–Mexico borderlands, Bartlett sketched the terrain, collected specimens of plants and animals and studied the languages, artifacts and cultures of the Southwestern Indians. He published his observations at his own expense in his *Personal Narrative*, a two-volume work that appeared in 1854 and remains a study of great scholarly merit. It is described by Robert V. Hine, a leading historian of the American West, as "a vivid, literate account of enduring value to scholars and naturalists." In 1968, Hine published a study of Bartlett's work entitled *Bartlett's West: Drawing the Mexican Boundary.*

In October 1853, Bartlett came back to Rhode Island with his ailing wife, Eliza, and their children. The timing of this return may have been related to Eliza's failing health; she died a few weeks after her arrival at her father's Pawtuxet home. During the next several months, Bartlett made provisions for the care of his youngest children, settled his accounts with the U.S. government and wrote essays for the *Providence Journal*.

In April 1855, he was placed on the Whig/American/Republican Party fusion ticket as a candidate for Rhode Island secretary of state. His nomination was undoubtedly the work of former governor and future U.S. senator Henry Bowen Anthony, a founder of the Republican Party and the *Providence Journal*'s publisher. In addition to Bartlett's outstanding qualifications, he was aided by the fact that Anthony had married Sarah Rhodes, Eliza's younger sister, and one of Bartlett's sons had been named Henry Anthony Bartlett. Here was a classic case of political nepotism that proved to have good results.

Bartlett won the April 1855 election and commenced a seventeen-year tenure in a post he would dramatically transform. He began immediately to organize, edit and publish the ten-volume *Records of the Colony of Rhode Island and Providence Plantations...1636–1792* (1855–1865), still the basic primary reference for Rhode Island's early history. Then, in succession, he published *A History of Lotteries in Rhode Island* (1856), *A Census of the Inhabitants of the Colony of Rhode Island* (1859), *A History of the Destruction of His Brittanic Majesty's Schooner Gaspee...* (1862), two indices to Rhode Island's early acts and resolves and the invaluable *Bibliography of Rhode Island* (1864), an annotated listing of all printed books, articles and pamphlets written about Rhode Island from its founding, prepared with assistance from Elisha Potter Jr. The Civil War gave rise to his books entitled *The Literature of the Rebellion* (a catalogue of works relating to that conflict) and *Memoirs of Rhode Island Officers Who Were Engaged in the Service of Their Country during the Great Rebellion of the South* (1867).

While serving as secretary of state, Bartlett also assisted John Carter Brown in compiling a catalogue of Brown's large collection of early Americana, which they titled *Bibliotheca Americana, A Catalog of Books Relating to North and South America in the Library of John Carter Brown, of Providence, R.I.*, a work still much used by the John Carter Brown Library's staff. After Bartlett relinquished the office of secretary of state in 1872 because his Republican Party failed to renominate him, he continued to work with Brown in the expansion of that remarkable library.

During the final fourteen years of his life, Bartlett traveled, compiled genealogies of the Wanton and Russell families of Rhode Island, continued his work (commenced in 1856) of developing a gallery of Rhode Island portraits at Brown University and enlarged a very sizable private library of his own, with concentrations in geography, ethnology, antiquities, philology, history and the classics. He also compiled large and elaborate scrapbooks relating to major current events, and he made numerous watercolor sketches of various Rhode Island scenes.

In 1874, as an active member of the Soldiers' National Cemetery Commission at Gettysburg, Bartlett produced a 109-page memorial volume for the laying of the cornerstone of the monument erected by that organization. In his *Autobiography*, skillfully and thoroughly edited by geomorphologist Jerry E. Mueller, Bartlett states that he was on the platform "within ten feet of Mr. Lincoln" when the president delivered his immortal address. In November 1863, shortly after that memorable event, Bartlett married Ellen E. Eddy, daughter of Nelson S. Eddy of Providence, the ancestor and namesake of the famed singer.

Bartlett's brilliant career ended with his death on May 28, 1886. He was survived by his second wife and was buried in the Bartlett family plot in Providence's Swan Point Cemetery. His memory and legacy survives, however, through the efforts of local historians and bibliophiles who honored him by creating the John Russell Bartlett Society in 1983.

# X

# THE REFORMERS

## SETH LUTHER

Of all the Rhode Island leaders profiled herein, no person's personal life was more erratic, peripatetic or tragic than that of Seth Luther. No one traveled through America as extensively or delivered more public addresses. No one lived in a more impoverished condition or fought as hard for the working class.

Luther was born in Providence sometime in 1795, one of at least four sons born to Rebecca and Thomas Luther, a leather tanner. His mother's maiden name is unknown, but his father, a Revolutionary War veteran, was descended from John Luther, one of the earliest settlers of nearby Taunton, Massachusetts.

Seth was educated in Providence common schools, read widely and obviously learned well because he became an articulate and inspiring orator and a knowledgeable writer. Unlike Tristam Burges, however, he was not destined to become a professor of oratory and belles-lettres; instead, he was apprenticed to prominent Providence builder Caleb Earle and learned the trade of a carpenter and housewright.

One of the apt words that could be used to describe Luther is "restless." In 1817, soon after reaching his majority, he undertook the first of his several trips to America's western frontier of settlement—Ohio, Indiana and Illinois—where he claimed to "have been delighted after a journey of 40 miles per day on foot, in the vast, gloomy, and grand forests of the West…to enter the hospitable log-cabin of the hardy pioneer…and listen to his well-told tale of hardships endured, of difficulties surmounted, and domestic happiness obtained through perseverance."

The Reformers

AN

# ADDRESS

ON THE

## RIGHT OF FREE SUFFRAGE,

DELIVERED BY THE REQUEST OF FREEHOLDERS AND OTHERS OF THE
CITY OF PROVIDENCE, RHODE-ISLAND, IN THE OLD TOWN HOUSE,
APRIL 19, AND REPEATED APRIL 26, AT THE SAME PLACE.

WITH AN

## APPENDIX,

CONTAINING THE

### RHODE-ISLAND BILL OF RIGHTS,

AND THE

#### REJECTED PETITION,

PRESENTED IN 1829, TO THE LEGISLATURE OF RHODE-ISLAND, BY NEARLY
2000 PETITIONERS, INCLUDING 700 FREEHOLDERS, WHO WERE
ALL DENOMINATED *VAGABONDS* AND *RENEGADES* BY

#### BENJAMIN HAZARD,

WHO REPORTED ON THAT PETITION TO THE GENERAL ASSEMBLY.

' We hold this truth to be self-evident, that all men are created equal.'

#### BY SETH LUTHER.

PROVIDENCE:
PRINTED BY S. R. WEEDEN.

### 1833.

Seth Luther wrote, delivered and published this reform-oriented *Address* in 1833. It helped to set the stage for the call of the state constitutional convention of 1834 and established an association between Luther and Thomas Wilson Dorr.

University of Rhode Island sociology professor Carl Gersuny, who has done more than anyone to document Luther's importance in America's early labor movement, has best described the impact on Luther of his contrasting impressions of the East and the West: "His mission in life was rooted in the stark contrast he perceived between…his encounters with egalitarian frontier hospitality and the rhetoric of the Revolution ('all men are created equal') and…the class inequities of the Northeast." Another sympathetic historian, Louis Hartz, styled Luther "a working-class rebel," and that assessment also hits the mark. When Luther was back in Providence after his initial venture, records indicate that he was expelled from the fellowship of the First Baptist Church and spent time in prison for debt.

Luther's earliest involvement with Rhode Island's movement for political and constitutional reform occurred at a large Providence rally in March 1829, where participants voiced opposition to Rhode Island's real estate (i.e., freehold) requirement for voting, office holding, jury duty and other civil rights. That group's resultant petition to the General Assembly was emphatically denied via a scathing report penned by Benjamin Hazard, an archconservative legislator from Newport.

Despite this rebuff, Luther continued his agitation on behalf of the workingman—a category that for him included women, children and the unskilled laborer—by delivering addresses throughout eastern New England and writing pro-labor essays. He was instrumental in the creation of the New England Association of Farmers and Mechanics in 1832 and the Boston Trades Union in 1834. His greatest impact, however, was in Rhode Island.

On April 19, 1833 (Patriot's Day), Luther helped to initiate another effort to achieve constitutional reform when he delivered two spirited public addresses at the Providence Town House on Benefit Street. These long exhortations were then printed as *An Address on the Right of Free Suffrage*, a pamphlet that anticipated the political philosophy of the Dorr Rebellion. This notable and influential *Address* was tainted by sarcasm, bombast, ridicule and irreverence, but its attack on Rhode Island's freehold was surprisingly learned and basically accurate. Luther loved to remind his audiences that he was "merely a poor journeyman carpenter," but despite such self-deprecation his address dared to blast the "small potato aristocrats" who were responsible for the perpetuation of a freehold system that was "contrary to the Declaration of Independence, the Constitution of the United States, the Bill of Rights of the State of Rhode Island, and the dictates of common sense."

Luther's fulminations against the suffrage statute reinforced those criticisms that had been voiced at the 1829 Providence rally, but his proposed method of securing relief was more drastic. To exert pressure on the legislature, he recommended that non-freemen refuse to pay taxes and decline to perform military duty. "No law…assessing a tax on non-voters, can with justice be collected; for they have never given their assent to the tax, directly or indirectly, by themselves or their representatives," he argued. "Resist tyranny, if need be, sword in hand."

Although he recommended "passive resistance" at the outset, the *Address*'s use of the aphorism "peaceably if we can, forcibly if we must," no doubt shook the complacency of the landed establishment. So also did Luther's assertion, anticipatory of Thomas Dorr, that the people possess "a right to assemble in primary meetings and appoint Delegates to a Convention" that has "a right to form a Constitution, and submit it" for ratification and adoption as "the law of the land." This bold course of bypassing the General Assembly was the one eventually pursued, but in 1833, hope for less impetuous change still existed and more moderate alternatives temporarily prevailed.

The Providence gathering to whom Luther appealed in April 1833, when he first delivered his *Address*, was an ad hoc association consisting mainly of "workingmen," who appointed a committee that evening to correspond with "friends in different parts of the State, for the purpose of fixing a time and place, for holding a State Convention." This committee, headed by William I. Tillinghast, a Providence barber, was composed of three freemen and three non-freemen. The other members of the group, who proudly added their names and occupations on all reports and correspondence, were Lawrence Richards, blacksmith; William Mitchell, shoemaker; Seth Luther, housewright; William Miller, currier; and David Brown, watch and clock maker.

The 1833 protest led to the call of a constitutional convention the following year, but this abortive gathering adjourned without drafting a new basic law. The 1834 convention, in which delegates were apportioned in replication of the conservative General Assembly, resisted change, despite the reform efforts therein of two young Providence attorneys, Joseph K. Angell and Thomas Wilson Dorr.

Between 1834 and 1840, Luther continued his far-flung travels, spreading the gospel of labor. In one surviving address to the mechanics and workingmen of Brooklyn on the Fourth of July 1836, he impressed upon his audience the fact that Jesus Christ was a carpenter and a workingman.

Sometimes wearied by his efforts, Luther occasionally returned to his father's home in Providence for rest and rejuvenation. However, when the Rhode Island Suffrage Association formed in the aftermath of the hectic "Log Cabin and Hard Cider" presidential campaign of 1840, he was back in the local fray, delivering reform speeches throughout the state. As Thomas Dorr emerged as the leader of this popular movement, Luther befriended him and became his unshakeable ally. He was with Dorr when the newly inaugurated people's governor attempted to take possession of the state arsenal at the Dexter Training Grounds after midnight on May 18, 1842, and he was with Dorr in Chepachet in late June, when the beleaguered reformer attempted to convene the people's legislature in this Glocester village.

After Dorr's followers fled Chepachet, rather than do battle with an advancing state militia force of 3,500, Governor Samuel Ward King declared martial law. Luther was arrested near the mill villages of Woonsocket Falls and brought to Providence with a score of other prisoners. According to his own testimony, "We were exhibited through the streets in triumph to glut the vengeance of the most cursed aristocracy that ever disgraced humanity." He was imprisoned on the day his eighty-seven-year-old father died, and he was denied the privilege of attending the funeral.

For his allegedly treasonous actions, Luther remained in prison until March 1843, first in Providence and then in Newport. He was represented by Dorr's close friend attorney Walter S. Burges. Luther made an attempt at escape in late 1842 by setting fire to his cell and rushing out of it when the jailer went for water, but he was quickly apprehended. When the state dropped its charges against him in August 1843, he traveled to Baltimore, where, according to Luther's account, sympathetic individuals, including Chief Justice Roger B. Taney, a Maryland native, raised a fund of forty dollars to enable him to visit a friend in rural Illinois, with whom he spent the winter of 1843–44.

During the presidential campaign of 1844, Luther traveled on foot throughout Ohio, Indiana, Michigan and Illinois, attempting to generate popular support for liberating the imprisoned Dorr under the slogan "Polk, Dallas, and Dorr." By mid-1845, after Dorr had been freed from jail, Luther was back in Providence for another brief stay. In letters to Dorr, he denounced the "false hearted friends" of the people's governor, those who failed to stand by "you and the cause" and "who forsook you in the darkest days of despair, some of whom are now fawning about you like puppies."

After another trip westward, Luther returned to New England in 1846 to campaign for the ten-hour workday. Then he suffered a mental breakdown. When the Mexican War erupted in May, he sent an unsolicited letter to President James K. Polk, offering his assistance as a clerk; in it, he claimed, with some hyperbole, to have traveled "about 150,000 miles, within thirty years, in the United States." Less than two weeks later, he was arrested, sword in hand, for attempting to rob a Boston bank by demanding "a thousand dollars in the name of President Polk."

On June 15, 1846, Luther was committed to a mental asylum in Cambridge, Massachusetts, and would remain institutionalized for the remainder of his life. In November of that year, he was transferred to the Dexter Asylum at the expense of the City of Providence, where he became a workhouse inmate. After Butler Hospital opened in December 1847, he was transferred there, and with Dr. Isaac Ray soon diagnosing him as "incurable," Luther remained at Butler until November 1858. During that time, no visitor came to see him. Burdened by the economic panic of 1857, the city decided to end the expense of his care at a time when the hospital began to discourage the presence of incurable pauper inmates. He was then transferred to the less expensive Vermont Asylum in Brattleboro, where he died on April 23, 1863, and was buried in a pauper's grave.

The relentless *Providence Journal*, which had attacked Luther through life, wrote a scathing obituary. While admitting that "he had considerable talent for both writing and speaking," the paper's parting shot was that "he was too violent, willful, and headstrong to accomplish any good" during "his worse than useless life." The bitter scribe who wrote that anonymous diatribe is long forgotten, but Luther's reform legacy lives on, especially through the efforts of URI professor Scott Molloy and his Rhode Island Labor History Society.

# GOVERNOR THOMAS WILSON DORR

Thomas Wilson Dorr was born in Providence on November 5, 1805, the eldest of the seven children of Sullivan Dorr, a wealthy merchant and business leader, and Lydia Allen, a prominent socialite and sister of noted inventor Zachariah Allen and governor and U.S. senator Philip Allen. Dorr, studious and dutiful as a youth, graduated with honors from Harvard in 1823, the second-ranking pupil in his class. He then studied law in New York City under Chancellor James Kent, passed the bar, toured the country, practiced law for a time in New York and returned to Providence in 1833 to begin a life of public service.

As a Whig state legislator (1834–37), the leader of a constitutional reform effort (1834–37), a Democratic state chairman (1840–41), a political insurrectionary (1842) and the leader of the Equal Rights wing of the Rhode Island Democratic Party (1842–54), Dorr was the catalyst that hastened the demise of the Royal Charter of 1663 and the adoption of a written state constitution. Ironically, neither document met with his approval, for his egalitarian philosophy was best expressed in the so-called People's Constitution, of which Dorr was the principal draftsman.

Governor Thomas
Wilson Dorr.

It was Dorr's attempt to put this constitution into effect by invoking his version of the Lockean doctrine of popular constituent sovereignty that precipitated the Dorr War in 1842. Dorr's political goals—"free suffrage" with no discrimination against the foreign-born, "one-man, one-vote," an independent judiciary, a more powerful and dynamic executive and the secret ballot—were not permanently achieved in Rhode Island during his lifetime, but they placed him in the front rank of the political reformers of Jacksonian America.

Late in December 1841, the progressive People's Constitution was approved in a three-day referendum by a majority of Rhode Island's free white adult males acting in defiance of the existing state authorities. In April 1842, Dorr, a reluctant candidate, was elected the "people's governor" under this new regime, and the state was confronted with two rival governments. Generally, urban Whigs and rural Democrats opposed the Dorrites and united to form the Law and Order Party. These conservatives prevailed, and after surrendering to them, Dorr was tried, convicted and imprisoned for treason against the state.

# The Reformers

Lydia Allen Dorr
(1782–1859) was the
mother of Governor
Thomas Wilson Dorr,
the mother-in-law of
House Speaker and chief
justice Samuel Ames, the
sister of Governor Philip
Allen and entrepreneur
Zachariah Allen and
the wife of merchant,
banker and businessman
Sullivan Dorr.

The Whig-led Law and Order coalition dominated state politics for the remainder of the decade, despite a brief intraparty dispute in 1845 over whether to liberate Dorr. Counting the time he spent awaiting trial, the vanquished reformer was actually confined to prison for a total of twenty months, an ordeal that shattered his fragile health and contributed to his political and physical demise. Dorr's liberation, finally achieved on June 27, 1845, stirred national interest and was a Democratic issue in the 1844 presidential campaign, as evidenced by the slogan "Polk, Dallas and Dorr."

Dorr's rebellion was no tempest in a teapot; it had national repercussions and has enduring significance. The most important and controversial domestic occurrence of the John Tyler administration, it eventually involved the president, both houses of Congress and the Supreme Court. Of even greater significance, the Rhode Island upheaval inspired the substantial contributions of John C. Calhoun, John L. O'Sullivan, Orestes Brownson, Joseph Story, Daniel Webster, Horace Greeley, Benjamin Hallett and others of similar stature to the theories of suffrage, majority rule, minority rights and constitutional government.

Much less known but no less significant were Dorr's economic and social concerns. Despite his patrician status, Dorr gradually evolved into a laissez-faire Democrat with a deep aversion toward economic privilege. As a young state legislator, he sponsored the first comprehensive statute regulating state banks, a measure that led to his break with the local Whig Party. The People's Constitution was permeated with Equal Rights (Locofoco) economic doctrine that sought to curb the abuses of special corporate "privileges" and monopoly grants from government.

Dorr was also a pioneer of free public education, and his People's Constitution made education a fundamental right. As a member, and then chairman, of the Providence School Committee (1836–42), he established that city's secondary school system and made significant improvements in teacher education, recruitment and certification, administrative reorganization and physical facilities. When the famed educational innovator Henry Barnard came to Rhode Island in 1843 and observed the workings of the Providence school system, he announced that his goal as state commissioner was to bring the schools in the other towns up to the standards established by Dorr in the city of Providence.

Dorr was intensely concerned with the status of minorities. His support of equal voting rights for Irish Catholic immigrants was exploited by his opponents and led to the breakup of his reform coalition. Though not an abolitionist, Dorr actively opposed slavery, urged civil rights for blacks and worked with the leaders of the American Anti-Slavery Society as a delegate to that group's national convention. Dorr, a bachelor, worked well with local women's rights leaders, and they played a major role in the agitation leading to his liberation from prison.

Beginning in 1851, Dorr's uncle, Philip Allen, the new leader of Rhode Island's reform Democrats, captured the governorship for three successive one-year terms because of the defection of the rural Democrats from the Law and Order Party. When the Allen faction (called "Dorr Democrats") pardoned Dorr, reversed his treason conviction and attempted to reenact the People's Constitution, the agrarians again defected. At this juncture, Know-Nothingism and the rise of the Republican Party produced a major political realignment in Rhode Island.

Dorr participated in the Equal Rights resurgence of the early 1850s as political strategist and advisor to his popular uncle. As the tide of reform began to ebb, he died in Providence on December 27, 1854, from respiratory problems aggravated by his twenty-month incarceration in damp, poorly ventilated prisons and was buried in a relatively modest family plot in Swan Point Cemetery.

# The Reformers

Dorr is best known as the determined leader of the Dorr Rebellion, Rhode Island's crisis in constitutionalism, but he was much more than merely a rebel or a political reformer. He was a man of quality education, high social standing and diverse intellectual and social interests.

Some American historians have suggested the name "Age of Egalitarianism" for the period from the mid-1820s to the mid-1850s because a passion for equality of opportunity was the overriding theme of political, social and economic activists. A more broadly based democracy, an assault on neomercantilism and government-granted privilege and a crusade for a more just, humane and upwardly mobile social order were hallmarks of the era. This was the first great age of American reform, and Dorr was in the midst of it as an archetypical Equal Rights proponent.

By the end of the turbulent 1850s, the Republicans, who revived the Law and Order coalition, dominated state politics and would continue to do so until the New Deal. The urban wing of the Democratic Party, appealing mainly to Equal Rights advocates and Irish Catholics, was consigned to minority status until well into the twentieth century. They enshrined Dorr as their hero, and in 1935, when the state's Democrats finally gained control of the governorship and both houses of the General Assembly via the "Bloodless Revolution" for the first time since 1854, Governor Theodore Francis Green justified the coup by telling a statewide radio audience that his party's success was inspired by "the spiritual presence of the patron saint of the Democratic Party in Rhode Island—Thomas Wilson Dorr!"

In addition to a recitation of cold, hard facts, a format necessitated by the very brief biographical profiles presented in this book, Thomas Dorr (like Roger Williams in *Rhode Island's Founders*, the precursor to this volume) merits an analytical assessment of his enduring impact on Rhode Island.

Thomas Wilson Dorr is the pivotal figure in Rhode Island history. He drew his heritage, training and moral values from the old order and applied them toward the betterment of the new. He exemplified the best traits attributed to old-stock Rhode Islanders: individualism, daring, defiance of unjust authority and a passion for democracy and self-determination. Simultaneously, he inaugurated the role of patrician reformer typified in the modern era by such Rhode Island statesmen as Theodore Francis Green (who admittedly drew inspiration from Dorr), Claiborne Pell and John Hubbard Chafee.

Dorr thus served as the bridge between early and modern Rhode Island, between old stock and new and between the charter government that served Rhode Island for 180 years and the present constitutional order.

More than any other person, he influenced the governmental transition from the old Royal Charter regime to a new political system based on a written constitution. And although his preferred basic law—the People's Constitution—was denied implementation, its provisions and principles were gradually incorporated into the Rhode Island Constitution throughout the century and a half since Dorr's defeat.

But Dorr was not merely a force for constitutional change; he was also the quintessential reformer of America's first great age of reformist activity. In the economic realm, he drafted and secured the enactment of the first statute in any state providing for governmental regulation of state-chartered banks, and he worked diligently for the abolition of imprisonment for debt. He might well be described as Rhode Island's first consumer advocate. Dorr also attacked neomercantilism, whereby the state granted special privileges and monopolies to private business corporations; such a practice, he declared, was a violation of equal rights. Dorr was a pioneer in his advocacy of an economic system regulated in the public interest—the modern regulated economy.

Dorr's reformist zeal also extended to the social order. He was an early member of the American Anti-Slavery Society, led by William Lloyd Garrison and Rhode Islander Arnold Buffum, and he fought, albeit unsuccessfully, to enfranchise blacks via the People's Constitution. His efforts were extolled, in the aftermath of his defeat, by the abolitionist poet John Greenleaf Whittier. Though Dorr despised slavery, eventually he came to believe that the demeanor and demands of the radical abolitionists could destroy the Union.

Governor Dorr also encouraged the involvement of women in the public sphere. His leadership of the People's Party in 1842 inspired the first large-scale involvement of Rhode Island women in the political process. Support of Dorr's cause and sympathy for him because of the harsh treatment accorded the deposed people's governor led women to undertake such unprecedented political activities as forming free-suffrage associations, raising funds for the relief of those imprisoned for supporting the people's government, staging rallies and clambakes in support of reform, organizing a campaign for Dorr's liberation and writing political and legal defenses of the people's movement, most notably *Might and Right* (1844) by Frances Harriet Whipple, who is profiled herein.

In addition, Dorr made a major contribution toward the development of free public education in Rhode Island, both as a state legislator, in which office he earmarked the famous federal deposit of 1836 for the permanent school fund, and as a member and then president of the Providence School Committee, where he played the leading role in implementing such modern improvements as the appointment of Providence's first superintendent of schools, the establishment of teacher certification and training programs, the creation of Rhode Island's first public high school and the construction of modern school facilities.

On the burning issue of foreign immigration, Dorr attacked the nativism of his day. As early as 1833, when nativist violence first erupted, he made a public appeal for toleration toward Roman Catholics. Dorr's exhortation to his fellow Rhode Islanders revealed his humanity:

> *It is quite time that a better state of feeling should prevail, and that narrow illiberal prejudices should be discarded. Whatever good the division into sects may have done, it is time that they should overlook the party lines behind which they have entrenched themselves, and extend to each other the hand of fellowship. If men cannot agree in religious opinions—and, from the constitution of the human mind, such an agreement can never exist— they certainly can agree to differ peaceably. There is a common ground of good will and charity on which they can and ought to meet as brethren.*

Consistent with his principles and pronouncements, Dorr befriended and defended the Irish Catholic immigrants of the 1840s, structuring the People's Constitution to give naturalized Irishmen equal rights to those of native-born citizens. He helped to organize the defense for John Gordon in the famous Amasa Sprague murder trial and then spoke against the death penalty meted out to this hapless Irish Catholic merchant of Spragueville.

Optimistic, articulate, concerned—these were among the qualities of Thomas Dorr. Belief in fundamental human goodness, the brotherhood of men and majoritarian rule were basic articles in his political creed. Liberty and equality were to him, as much as to any reformer of this remarkable age, the indispensable conditions of human activity.

Dorr's 1843 lament—"All is lost save honor"—may well have been the story of his rebellion and his life, but it is neither his legacy nor the ultimate verdict of history. At the conclusion of his trial for treason, Dorr made an impassioned plea: "From the sentence of the court I appeal to the People of our State and of our Country. They shall decide between us. I commit myself without distrust to their final award." To his credit—and to ours—the confidence of this optimistic, if somewhat naive, Democrat continues to experience an inexorable, though painfully gradual, vindication in Rhode Island. In the many decades since his defeat and death, the judgment against him from Justice Job Durfee's biased court has been properly overruled by time and experience.

## HARRIET WARE

Harriet Ware was born on July 12, 1799, in Paxton, Massachusetts, a small town just northwest of Worcester and about thirteen miles northeast of the town of Ware, settled by her ancestors. Little is known about her formative years. The brief sketch of her life by her benefactor, the Reverend Francis Wayland, president of Brown University, is platitudinous and lacking in detail, but it does include a number of her personal letters. Consistent with the intense religious fervor of its author and his subject, it was published in 1853 by the American Sunday School Union. From it, we learn that Harriet was "gay and thoughtless, and wholly devoted to the pursuit of pleasure" in her teens, but in 1819, while a resident of Franklin, Massachusetts, she experienced a dramatic spiritual conversion so that "the whole force of her character was now turned in a new direction. Her renunciation of the world was sincere and universal."

Harriet Ware.

According to Wayland's memoir and her letters, we learn that Harriet Ware taught school in Union, Maine, and Hopkinton, Rhode Island, before coming to Providence in the spring of 1832. She was invited to the newly incorporated city by a "society of benevolent ladies" to create a Sunday school in the India Point-Fox Point section of Providence along its then busy waterfront. Inhabited by mariners, dockworkers and tradesmen, the area also contained an increasing number of Irish Catholic immigrants, causing Foxes Hill, overlooking the harbor, to be referred to as "Corky Hill." According to Wayland, it was "the most neglected spot in Providence," and Harriet's "motive for going there was to do good for those whom all other persons believed to be irreclaimable." According to Ware herself, she was told "that the people were completely savage, that it was an improper place for a female."

Although this terrifying assessment was obviously exaggerated by the East Side elite, Harriet Ware had no Sunday school picnic in her new position, yet her courage and persistence brought forty children to the school after its first year. Her success under adverse conditions prompted President Wayland and some of the benevolent ladies to offer financial assistance to give Ware's social experiment a fair trial, and several, including Lucy Wayland, the wife of the Brown president, even volunteered their services to ensure its success. Soon, the Sunday school added a primary school and a children's shelter.

By 1835, Ware's efforts had resulted in the chartering of a pioneering private institution that she named the Providence Children's Friend Society. This agency embraced "all children who are in the condition of orphanage" and was the only Rhode Island institution where provision was made for their support and education. Within a year, this facility housed thirteen boys and twenty-seven girls. Some were placed into good Protestant foster homes, while others remained at the orphanage until they reached their majority. The "unruly" were sometimes transferred to the Dexter Asylum (Providence's poor farm) or apprenticed out. To track its progress and gain further support, the society issued interesting annual reports detailing its efforts and describing the status of children under its care.

There is no doubt about Ware's zeal, integrity, dedication and commitment. The home was literally her mission in every sense of that word. However, with the number of Irish Catholic immigrants increasing during the 1840s, priests became alarmed that the Catholic children served by such an agency might be lost to the faith unless a Catholic orphanage was established. For this purpose, Bishop Bernard O'Reilly invited Mother Frances Xavier Warde and her Sisters of Mercy to Providence in 1851 to staff the new St.

Aloysius Home, as the Catholic counterpart to the Children's Friend Society was named.

Ware continued her benevolent efforts until she became gravely ill in 1847. Even when she was faced with terminal illness, her main concern was the enlargement of her orphanage to accommodate more needy children; when that goal was met, she confided to a friend that "now I feel that all my work is done." She died peacefully at her cherished home on June 26, 1847, less than three weeks before her forty-eighth birthday.

Professor Sandra Enos of Bryant University, an authority on the history of child welfare, assesses Harriet Ware's significance as follows: "In her founding of Children's Friend, Ware's leadership is emblematic of the social entrepreneur—vision, the talent to inspire, persistence, resourcefulness, the ability to adapt, and finally, the commitment and courage to be of service." Her work continues today as the Children's Friend and Services of Providence.

## ARNOLD BUFFUM AND ELIZABETH BUFFUM CHACE

Arnold Buffum, one of Rhode Island's leading abolitionists, was the second son among the eight children of William Buffum and Lydia Arnold. He was born on December 13, 1782, and raised in a farmhouse near Smithfield's Union Village, now part of North Smithfield. Arnold's childhood home, called the William Buffum House for his Quaker father who built it, still stands at 383 Great Road. William Buffum, a member of the Providence Society for Promoting the Abolition of Slavery, was a strong influence on his son Arnold.

Despite his rural roots and meager education, Arnold Buffum became an entrepreneur whose main business was the manufacture and sale of hats in Providence. He also patented some inventions pertaining to his trade and raised sheep on his father's farm as a source of felt for his hats. Business reverses during his career caused his relocation back to the family homestead, and then to Fall River and Philadelphia, and business interests even prompted him to visit Europe twice. He and his wife, the former Rebecca Gould, were married in 1803 and became the parents of seven children, all of whom were raised in the Quaker faith. The most notable of these children were their daughter Elizabeth and their son Edward, who became the Paris correspondent of the *New York Herald*.

Arnold Buffum's Quaker beliefs greatly influenced his views on slavery, and soon after William Lloyd Garrison began the publication of the *Liberator*

Arnold Buffum,

Elizabeth Buffum Chace.

in 1831, the two joined with other like-minded reformers to establish the New England Anti-Slavery Society in 1832. Garrison became the bold new organization's secretary-treasurer, while the eloquent Buffum was selected president and the group's first roving lecturer, a post not conducive to his economic well-being.

For the next decade and a half, Buffum traveled in New England, New York, New Jersey, Pennsylvania, Ohio and Indiana, preaching the gospel of abolitionism to all who would listen and especially to meetings of the Society of Friends. By the late 1830s, however, he broke with Garrison to support "political abolitionism" through the creation of a third party dedicated to that goal. He accordingly assisted James G. Birney in founding the Liberty Party in 1840 and supported the Free-Soil campaign of 1848. In addition to his passion against slavery, Buffum has also been described as a temperance advocate and a "lover of books."

In 1843, a fellow passenger on one of Buffum's European trips described him as "an Old Hickory [i.e., Jacksonian] abolitionist…a tall, gray-headed, gold-spectacled patriarch…a very sharp old fellow [who] has all his facts ready…abuses his country outrageously" for being proslavery but who is still a "genuine democratic American." In 1854, Buffum died near Perth Amboy, New Jersey, in Eagleswood, the utopian community founded by his daughter Rebecca Buffum Spring and her husband, Marcus Spring, but he was eventually returned home to the Smithfield Meetinghouse for burial beside his wife, Rebecca.

Arnold Buffum's reform work had a great influence on his second child, Elizabeth, born in Providence on Benefit Street on December 9, 1806. In 1828, she married fellow Quaker abolitionist Samuel Chace, a Fall River textile manufacturer. Elizabeth first became publicly active in the cause of abolition in 1835 when she and her two sisters, Lucy and Rebecca, helped to organize the Fall River Female Anti-Slavery Society, a group that allied with the radical wing of the antislavery movement led by William Lloyd Garrison. The Chaces continued their abolitionist efforts after moving to the Valley Falls section of Cumberland in 1840. Elizabeth organized antislavery meetings and brought illustrious abolitionists to address them, including Garrison, Sojourner Truth, Lucy Stone, Abbey Kelley and Wendell Phillips, and she made her home a station on the Underground Railroad. She detailed these activities in an 1891 book entitled *Antislavery Reminiscences*.

After the enactment of the Thirteenth Amendment abolishing slavery, Elizabeth Chace joined with Paulina Wright Davis to found the Rhode Island Women's Suffrage Association in 1868. Chace used her position as president of this organization to address the needs of Rhode Island's disadvantaged women and children, and she led the successful drive for the creation of the state Home and School for Dependent Children that was established in 1885. In the mid-1860s, she became a co-founder of the Free Religious Association and an influential temperance advocate. She also urged reforms to benefit factory workers, especially women and children operatives, as well as prisoners and other deprived groups. She was outspoken, indefatigable and relentless in advancing the reforms that she espoused, earning for herself the soubriquet the "conscience of Rhode Island."

Chace accomplished her noble deeds despite the great burdens and sorrows of motherhood. She and her husband had ten children in the years between 1830 and 1852, the first five of whom died of childhood diseases before the next five were born. Among those who did survive was their son Arnold Buffum Chace, the eleventh chancellor of Brown University and a renowned mathematician and Egyptologist. Even today, their progeny are locally prominent in the fields of business and education.

Elizabeth Chace's long life of reform ended in December 1899, but the memory of her achievements in Rhode Island and elsewhere persists. In 2002, she was selected as the first woman to be memorialized with a statue in the Rhode Island Statehouse, a recognition for local women long overdue.

A full, though dated, account of Chace's public life, which spanned over sixty years, is *Elizabeth Buffum Chace, 1806–1899: Her Life and Its Environment* (two volumes, 1914), written by her daughter Lillie Buffum Chace Wyman and Arthur Crawford Wyman, Elizabeth's grandson. Elizabeth C. Stevens, the editor of *Rhode Island History* magazine, provides a more recent and scholarly account in *Elizabeth Buffum Chace and Lillie Chace Wyman: A Century of Abolitionist, Suffragist, and Workers' Rights Activism* (2003).

# George T. Downing

In Rhode Island, slavery was placed on the road to extinction on March 1, 1784, when the General Assembly passed a gradual manumission act making any black born to a slave mother after that date free. Those who were slaves at that time had to be manumitted by their masters. Five such slaves were listed in the federal census of 1840, and not until the implementation of the state constitution of 1843 was slavery banned outright in Rhode Island. Free blacks with real estate could vote until 1822, when they were deprived of suffrage by statute. This restriction was erased by the constitution of 1843, in

George T. Downing.

part to reward blacks for their support of the prevailing Law and Order government.

With blacks politically impotent, socially ostracized, educationally segregated and some still enslaved during most of the decades covered by this book, it is understandable that very few black leaders emerged in Rhode Island during the antebellum era. George Thomas Downing was one notable exception.

Downing was born in New York City on December 30, 1819. His father, Thomas, was a native of coastal Virginia, and his mother, Rebecca West, came from Philadelphia. George, the eldest child, had three brothers and a sister. He was fortunate in that his father established a very upscale and successful New York City restaurant, whose patrons included many of the prominent businessmen and politicians of the metropolis. This success allowed George to attend private school, as well as the Mulberry Street School, where he met several young boys who would soon become vocal abolitionists, like George himself. When he was only fourteen, George and his black schoolmates—James McCune Smith, Henry Garnet, Alexander Crummel and Charles and Patrick Benson—formed a literary society and also discussed racial issues in America. At one of their meetings, they agreed not to celebrate the Fourth of July because it was "a perfect mockery" for African Americans.

George displayed such intellectual and leadership potential that his father sent him to Hamilton College in Clinton, New York, where he met and married Serena Leanora de Grasse, the daughter of a German mother and a father from India. Upon his return from Clinton, he joined with his father not only in the food business but also in the business of promoting racial justice. Both became active in the Underground Railroad, personally helping several fugitive slaves escape to freedom, and they lobbied the New York legislature to grant equal suffrage to blacks. Then, George struck out on his own.

In 1846, he came to Newport, a town that had a sizable black community, to replicate his father's oyster-house restaurant. This enterprise proved successful in a town that had begun to emerge as a fashionable summer resort and was attracting some of his father's New York patrons. Downing wasted little time expanding his operations. In 1850, he moved temporarily to Providence, where he established a catering business for that city's polite society. Then he turned his attention again to Newport, and in 1854–55, with some financing from his father, he built his impressive Sea Girt House on South Touro Street (now part of Bellevue Avenue), nearly opposite the Newport Tower. The multistory Sea Girt House included his residence, a restaurant, his catering business and "accommodations for gentlemen boarders." A suspicious fire destroyed the elegant building in 1860, but Downing was able to recover $40,000 of insurance proceeds to rebuild a larger structure on the site, which came to be called the Downing Block. During the Civil War, he rented its upper floor to the temporarily relocated U.S. Naval Academy as an infirmary.

Downing's business success, remarkable as it was, would not confer Hall of Fame status on him, but his successful campaigns against slavery and school desegregation in Rhode Island do earn him that distinction. He vigorously opposed the African colonization plan supported by Thomas Hazard, but he assisted the efforts of local abolitionists, such as the Buffums, and national leaders of this movement, like Massachusetts senator Charles Sumner and ex-slave Frederick Douglass. Although somewhat of a black elitist, Downing regarded himself as evidence of a black person's ability to succeed and prosper if afforded education and the equal opportunity to do so.

In his quest for human rights, Downing was most uniquely associated with the desegregation of Rhode Island's public schools, a campaign he commenced in 1855 with the support of Senator Sumner. By 1857, he had begun to take bold public action, launching a lobbying campaign, which he personally financed, against segregated education. Among other arguments, Downing appealed to the white leadership of the state by reminding them not only of the heroics of Rhode Island's black regiment during the Revolutionary War but also of the assistance that blacks had rendered to the victorious Law and Order Party during the Dorr Rebellion. Such rhetoric did not sit well with Rhode Island's Irish Catholics, but constitutional restrictions on their suffrage kept those residents of the state politically impotent.

Downing's desegregation campaign had some near misses, but it took the ratification of the Thirteenth Amendment in 1865 to overcome the resistance of such communities as Providence, Bristol and Downing's own Newport. Downing's oft-repeated argument was that all race distinctions stemmed from slavery, and thus they must die with slavery. In 1866, eleven years after Downing first strategized with Sumner, the General Assembly, with little debate, overwhelmingly voted to outlaw separate schools and ended the era of legal educational segregation in Rhode Island.

Downing continued his racial-equality crusade in the decades following the Civil War. In 1869, he helped to form the Colored National Labor Union because of the refusal of the all-white National Labor Union to admit blacks. By the late 1870s, he had become disenchanted with the Republican Party for abandoning Reconstruction and criticized what he called "the blind adhesion of the colored people to one party." He failed, however, in three attempts to secure election as a Newport Democrat to the Rhode Island General Assembly, leaving the honor of becoming the state's first African American legislator to the Reverend Mahlon Van Horne, a Newport Republican, who was elected to the House for three consecutive one-year terms, beginning in 1885.

Downing's most visible job mixed his two passions: food and politics. For twelve years, from 1865 to 1877, the outspoken Downing was in charge of the café dining room of the U.S. House of Representatives, giving him the opportunity to influence and lobby policymakers. One salutary project on which he worked was the passage in 1873 of an equal-opportunity public accommodations law for the District of Columbia. Two years after leaving his post in Washington, he retired from his Newport business.

George Downing died at his Newport home on July 21, 1903, surrounded by his several children, one of whom, Serena, wrote his brief biography in 1910. At his passing, the *Boston Globe* called him "the foremost colored man in the country" and praised his efforts on behalf of liberty and equality for all Americans.

# THOMAS ROBINSON HAZARD

Thomas Robinson Hazard was a South Kingstown manufacturer, agriculturalist, author and social reformer who embodied the egalitarian spirit of the pre–Civil War age of reform. Affectionately called "Shepherd Tom" because of his prize sheep herd, Hazard, born on January 3, 1797,

Thomas Robinson Hazard, with his family.

was a seventh-generation descendant of Thomas Hazard, the progenitor of the famous Hazard clan of Rhode Island and one of the nine founders of Newport. Shepherd Tom was also the grandson of Thomas Hazard (1720–1798), an eighteenth-century South County Quaker abolitionist called College Tom because of his advanced study at Yale, and the older brother of Rowland Gibson Hazard (1801–1888), a noted Peace Dale woolen manufacturer, railroad promoter, financial expert and writer on philosophical subjects. The parents of these Hall of Fame brothers were Mary Peace and Rowland Hazard Sr., who established a woolen mill and the village he called Peace Dale in 1802, when Thomas was five years old.

Despite his family's prominence, Thomas had limited formal education except for his four-year attendance at a Quaker boarding school in Westtown, Pennsylvania. Upon his return to Rhode Island, he learned the textile business from his father at the Peace Dale Mill, and at the age of twenty-four he purchased his own waterpower site nearby and received a gift of seventy prime acres of pastureland from his father. Adjacent to his own woolen mill, the pasture transformed the young entrepreneur into Shepherd Tom as his flock of sheep grew to more than 1,200 in size. As a mill owner, he prospered greatly, and at the somewhat advanced age of forty-one, he married Frances Minturn, a New Yorker, described by contemporaries as "a highly cultured lady of great personal beauty." Unlike his brother Rowland and the other entrepreneurs profiled herein, Shepherd Tom could walk away from business activities to pursue a leisurely but very significant life dedicated to learning and social reform.

In 1840, he returned to his family's Aquidneck Island roots and purchased a seventeen-acre estate called Vaucluse on Middletown's eastern shore, overlooking the Sakonnet River. Its setting inspired him to publish several articles on horticulture. In this idyllic spot, he and his wife raised six children prior to her death in 1854 at the age of forty-two. Tragically, her death was preceded by that of two of their young daughters.

Immediately upon his retirement, this ardent Whig assumed the role of patrician reformer. Like his fellow Quakers, he abhorred slavery. His solution, similar to the one advocated by Jefferson, Madison and Monroe, was to free the slaves and colonize them in Liberia, back to their roots. To that end, he became an active member and vice-president of the African Colonization Society.

Most of his reform impulses, however, proved more constructive and successful. In 1856, he published *A Constitutional Manual: Negro Slavery and the Constitution*, urging both an end to slavery and the preservation of the Union. He was also a strong advocate of education. In 1821, he became the first manufacturer to establish an evening school for workers in his mill and, in 1851, took the lead in establishing the Rhode Island Institute of Instruction, the forerunner of Rhode Island College. In the late 1840s, Thomas spearheaded local relief efforts for victims of the Irish potato famine, including a generous donation of his own.

Thomas and his brother Rowland supported the establishment of Butler Hospital in Providence, and Thomas's involvement with that project led him to make a report to the General Assembly in 1851 on the condition of the poor and the insane in every town in Rhode Island, except for New Shoreham. This exposé influenced the reform-oriented Dorr Democrats, then in control of the legislature, to institute improvements in the care and management of the poor, the insane, the blind, the deaf and the dumb and to make regular annual appropriations for such purposes.

Another of Thomas Hazard's notable contributions to the General Assembly came in 1852, when he provided the Dorr Democrats with a petition and a forty-page report praying for the abolition of capital punishment in Rhode Island, a request inspired by the unjust execution of Irish immigrant John Gordon on February 14, 1845, for the murder of Amasa Sprague. In concert with Attorney General Walter S. Burges, state senator Thomas Davis and representatives Ariel Ballou, John Weeden and others, Hazard helped to secure a law banning the death penalty. Although Hazard never held public office of any kind, he took a deep interest in many areas of societal reform and used his pen, without fear or favor, toward any cause he felt to be just.

After his wife's death, Hazard turned his avid attention to spiritualism and began to seek solace in séances. He also wrote a number of articles on the spiritualistic belief that the dead communicate with the living, a view devoutly held by some of Rhode Island's leading female authors, such as Frances (Whipple) McDougall and Sarah Helen Whitman. In 1870, he compiled the *Ordeal of Life* based on information gathered by medium John C. Grinnell from his encounters with 1,500 spirits.

Hazard also turned to more traditional historical and genealogical writing. In 1879, he published *Recollections of Olden Times,* a work that casts a rich afterglow on nineteenth-century life in South County while also providing genealogies of the fascinating Hazard and Robinson families. The *Jonny-Cake Papers of "Shepherd Tom,"* a collection of newspaper articles relating to South County's nineteenth-century customs and traditions, was published posthumously in 1915 by his grand-niece Caroline Hazard, a president of Wellesley College.

Thomas Robinson Hazard died in New York City on March 26, 1886, at the age of eighty-nine. His remains were returned to his estate at Vaucluse for burial beside his wife.

## CONGRESSMAN THOMAS DAVIS AND PAULINA (KELLOGG) WRIGHT DAVIS

Thomas Davis was born in Dublin, Ireland, on December 18, 1806. He attended private schools in Ireland and migrated to America in 1817, settling in Providence. Becoming a pioneer in Rhode Island's jewelry industry, he amassed sufficient wealth to enable him to finance a variety of political, civic and reform endeavors. Little is known about his first marriage; his wife, Eliza Jones Chace, died in December 1840 at the age of thirty.

Davis became a state senator from Providence, serving from 1845 to 1853, and he emerged as a leader of the reform wing of the Democratic Party led by Thomas Wilson Dorr. As a member of the General Assembly, Davis played a leading role in the passage of the 1852 act banning the death

Congressman Thomas Davis.

Paulina (Kellogg) Wright Davis.

penalty in Rhode Island, and he was a strong advocate of constitutional reform. Though he was a Unitarian, he campaigned vigorously for the removal of the real estate requirement for voting and office holding required of naturalized citizens in the state, most of whom were Catholic Irish. As a humanitarian, he was an ardent abolitionist and a leader in Rhode Island's relief effort during Ireland's Great Famine.

In 1853, the Dorr Democrats sent Governor Philip Allen to the United States Senate and nominated Davis as their congressional candidate from the Eastern District. Davis defeated Whig candidate George G. King by a margin of 5,524 to 4,942, but although Davis was elected, the presence of a Free-Soil candidate in the race narrowed his required majority to 175 votes. In 1855, Davis was soundly defeated in his reelection bid by the American (Know-Nothing) Party candidate, Tiverton farmer Nathaniel B. Durfee, who then easily dispatched Democrat Ambrose E. Burnside of Bristol when Durfee ran for reelection in 1857 as a Republican.

Davis lost his run for reelection in part because he broke with his party by openly opposing Stephen Douglas's Kansas-Nebraska Act, a measure that opened the U.S. territories to the possibility of slavery, but he was also a victim of the native American hysteria that swept the country in the mid-1850s. Despite the growing unpopularity of his reform views, he spoke out courageously. In an 1855 Newport address, immigrant Davis denounced the Know-Nothing Party's "persecution of foreign born citizens," describing that party as "a conspiracy against the rights of man" and expressing his extreme displeasure with Durfee's attacks on Roman Catholics. Undaunted by his 1855 defeat, Davis made four more attempts to regain his congressional seat in 1859, 1870, 1872 and 1878, all of which were unsuccessful.

By the late 1850s, the national Democratic Party's tolerance of slavery prompted Davis to become a Republican, but his pro-Irish stance incurred the wrath of Republican leader Henry Bowen Anthony, a U.S. senator, archnativist, founder of the Republican Party and editor of the *Providence Journal*. When Davis sought election to Congress as a Republican in 1859, he was defeated by Christopher Robinson, an American-Republican fusion candidate whom Anthony sponsored. This "treachery," as Davis called it, together with the differences between Davis and Anthony regarding the real estate voting qualification for naturalized citizens, prompted a bitter feud. The most vitriolic example of this long-running mutual contempt was a thirty-three-page "open letter" from Davis to Anthony in 1866 entitled "Rhode Island Politics and Journalism," where, among other insults, Davis referred to Anthony as a man of "baseness and treachery" and "an apostate politician of unscrupulous character." By the time of his 1872 campaign for Congress, Davis had been prompted by Anthony's leadership role in the Republican Party to return to the much more reform-oriented Democratic fold.

Despite his lack of success on the federal level, Davis again served in the state senate (1877–78) and then became a state representative (1887–90), as well as a member of the Providence School Committee. In a supremely ironic twist, the naturalized Davis temporarily lost his right to vote and hold office in 1880 when his jewelry business failed. Needless to say, however, he became a leader in the statewide Equal Rights movement of the 1880s, a reform campaign that resulted in the abandonment of the real estate voting requirement via the Bourne Amendment of 1888.

Notwithstanding his several political positions, Congressman Davis's principal legacies were as a reformer, a patron of the arts and a philanthropist. In concert with his second wife, Paulina, he hosted cultural gatherings at each of his two Providence residences—a Greek revival house at 503–507 Chalkstone Avenue, dating from 1850, and then at a stately Gothic mansion built in 1869 on a hilltop near the junction of Chalkstone Avenue and Raymond Street in a thirty-four-acre parklike setting. At the salons hosted by Thomas and Paulina, intellectuals, artists and reformers from around the region came to discuss the vital issues of the day.

Thomas Davis's charming and intelligent second wife was born in Bloomfield, New York, on August 7, 1813, the daughter of Captain Ebenezer Kellogg and Polly Saxon. After the deaths of both parents, Paulina was raised by a strict orthodox Presbyterian aunt. After a brief immersion with religion, Paulina married Francis Wright, a wealthy Utica merchant, in 1833. The couple became very involved in various contemporary reforms, especially abolitionism and women's rights.

Her husband's death in 1845 left Paulina Wright desolate, but she was wealthy and free to embark on a career as a lecturer and women's health advocate. She studied medicine in New York City and lectured widely on female anatomy and physiognomy. While on tour in Providence, Paulina met widower Thomas Davis, who held reform sentiments similar to hers. The couple married in April 1849 and began a partnership that exerted great influence on Rhode Island's social and cultural life during the mid-nineteenth century. Paulina hosted numerous gatherings on the Davises' spacious Providence estate in such a manner that she inspired one observer to describe her as "a radiant figure" in her "circle of literary, artistic, and reformatory people."

Paulina Davis worked on the National Women's Rights Convention held in Worcester in 1850, and two years later she launched the publication of *Una*, which she called the first women's magazine devoted to "the elevation of women." She was determined to promote a dialogue among women on the issues of labor, marriage, suffrage, property rights and education, but *Una* had a short lifespan.

In 1866, Paulina Davis made many of the arrangements for the twentieth-anniversary meeting of the women's suffrage movement held in New York City, and in 1871 she published the proceedings of that gathering as *The History of the National Women's Rights Movement*. During the 1860s and 1870s, she traveled abroad, meeting many prominent European reformers and indulging her love and skill for art by copying the paintings of great masters. She abandoned her artwork only when she became crippled with arthritis.

Paulina Davis died in Providence on August 24, 1876, shortly after observing her sixty-third birthday. Congressman Thomas Davis died on July 26, 1895, at the age of eighty-eight and was laid to rest in Swan Point Cemetery beside his equally illustrious wife and his first wife, Eliza.

In 1891, the City of Providence purchased the Davis estate at a bargain price for recreational use, and enlarging the tract, it created Davis Park. In 1945, the federal government condemned the land, demolished the mansion and built the Veterans' Administration Hospital, but the flat low-lying area to the east of the facility was then returned to the city, which uses it presently as a ball field and playground.

# Appendix
# RHODE ISLANDERS AND
# THE NATION

S ixteen additional inductees to the Rhode Island Heritage Hall of Fame are noted here, rather than with a full profile, because their direct impact on the "making of modern Rhode Island" was slight and overshadowed by their exploits elsewhere. Despite their Rhode Island birth or residence, their greatness or fame was achieved beyond the confines of tiny Rhode Island.

One of the striking aspects of this list of expatriate Rhode Island members of its Hall of Fame is the number of them associated with Newport. Ten of them were either born or raised in the "City by the Sea" or summered there regularly. Newport's economic stagnation after the British occupation during the American Revolution, the city's naval heritage and its proximity to Boston as a site for professional advancement account for most of Newport's outmigration; its rise to prominence as a fashionable resort for the rich and the cultured explains the presence of Bancroft, Moore and later Hall of Fame members such as Julia Ward Howe.

GEORGE BANCROFT (October 3, 1800–January 17, 1891) was born in Worcester, Massachusetts, and educated at Harvard and in Germany. He became America's greatest nineteenth-century historian. His magnum opus was his ultranationalistic, deeply researched ten-volume *History of the United States*, begun in 1834 and completed in 1874. An ardent Democrat, he was appointed secretary of the navy in 1845 by James Knox Polk and was instrumental in establishing the U.S. Naval Academy, which actually came from Annapolis to Newport during the Civil War. Later in life, Bancroft served as U.S. minister to England and minister to Prussia, where he had studied as a youth. He was a prominent member of Newport's famed summer colony from 1851 until his death, and he maintained a Cliff Walk home there and became an expert horticulturalist; his expertise with roses helped to create a strain called the American Beauty Rose. Bancroft's house was later demolished by Hermann and Theresa Fair Oelrichs, who built their mansion on the site, retaining for it the name of Bancroft's home, Rosecliff. The historian died in Washington and was buried in his native Worcester.

REVEREND WILLIAM ELLERY CHANNING (April 7, 1780–October 2, 1842) was born in Newport, a grandson of William Ellery, a Rhode Island signer of the Declaration of Independence. He was also raised in Newport prior to graduating from Harvard in 1798. Thereafter, he often visited Rhode Island, but he made his career in Boston as America's foremost minister of Unitarianism, a sect that rejected harsh Calvinistic theology in favor of a gentle, loving relationship with God. From 1803 until his death, Channing was pastor of Boston's Federal Street Church. His sermons and writings on religious reform and abolitionism had great influence, and his thought contributed to the development of the Transcendentalist movement in New England. He died in 1842 and is buried in Mount Auburn Cemetery in Cambridge, Massachusetts. A monument to his memory graces Newport's Touro Park.

DR. WALTER CHANNING (April 15, 1786–July 27, 1876) was born in Newport, the younger brother of the Reverend William Ellery Channing. Like his brother, he studied at Harvard and made his career in Boston, but as a noted physician and professor of medicine. After graduating from the medical school of the University of Pennsylvania in 1809, he became Harvard's first professor of obstetrics and medical jurisprudence and, from 1819 to 1847, the dean of its medical school. In 1846, he became one of the first American physicians to employ anesthesia (ether) during childbirth and other operations. In the course of his long career, he published numerous essays on medicine and medical history. He died at his home in Brookline, Massachusetts.

PRUDENCE CRANDALL (September 3, 1803–January 28, 1890) was born in Hopkinton, Rhode Island, the daughter of Pardon Crandall, a Quaker farmer, and Esther Carpenter. She was educated at Moses Brown School in Providence. In 1831, some leading citizens of Canterbury, Connecticut, where her family had moved, hired Crandall to organize a school for girls. Her Canterbury Female Seminary opened and ran smoothly until the fall of 1832, when Sarah Harris, the daughter of a prosperous African American farmer, sought admission, and Prudence accepted her. This act precipitated a controversy of national proportions. When local whites withdrew their daughters, Crandall boldly reorganized the school in 1833 as a teacher-training institution for young black women. She persisted despite harassment, boycotts and threats of violence. Soon, frustrated townsmen set fire to the school, forcing its closure in September 1834. Abolitionist leaders seized upon this brief but volatile incident, and Crandall became a national symbol in their crusade against slavery and racial intolerance. After this episode, Crandall left Connecticut, moving first to New York, then to Illinois and ultimately to Kansas, where she died in 1890 at the age of eighty-six.

JOHN DEWOLF (September 6, 1779–March 8, 1872) was a member of the famous and wealthy clan of Bristol merchants. Although Captain Robert Gray of Tiverton (see *Rhode Island Founders*) became the first American to circumnavigate the globe in 1790 aboard his ship *Columbia*, John DeWolf became the first American (and probably the first human) to travel around the world by crossing Asia overland, a remarkable journey detailed in his published diary, *A Voyage to the North Pacific and a Journey Through Siberia More Than Half-a-Century Ago* (1861). In this narrative, "Northwest John" (as he was called) describes his voyage aboard DeWolf's ship *Juno*, which departed Bristol on August 13, 1804, to sail around Cape Horn to acquire furs along the north Pacific Coast. After accumulating a full cargo of pelts, DeWolf reached Russian Alaska in May 1805. Here he sold the *Juno* to the Russian America Company and sent a quantity of furs back to Bristol in a sister ship. After spending two years among the Russian traders and trappers, John crossed the Bering Strait and set off across Siberia via foot, sled, boat and horseback, reaching St. Petersburg on October 21, 1807. After leaving Russia, he encountered in Denmark the ship *Mary* out of Portland, Maine, and sailed on it back to America after a stopover in Liverpool, England. DeWolf finally arrived in Bristol on April Fool's Day 1808, almost forty-four months after he had departed on the *Juno*. Thereafter, John DeWolf lived a relatively unspectacular life and died at the home of his daughter in Dorchester, Massachusetts, on March 8, 1872.

CHARLES BIRD KING (September 26, 1785–March 18, 1862) was born in Newport, the only child of Deborah Bird and Revolutionary War veteran Captain Zebulon King, who moved the family to Ohio in 1789 and was killed there by Indians. When Charles King was fifteen, he went to New York to study portrait painting, and he then journeyed to London, where he was taught by Benjamin West at the Royal Academy. After returning to America in 1812, he eventually settled in Washington, D.C., where he was able to paint the portraits of two presidents (Monroe and J.Q. Adams) and many noted politicians. His most notable works, however, are the 143 portraits he painted of Native American delegations that came to Washington under the auspices of the U.S. Bureau of Indian Affairs between 1822 and 1842, a collection that became known as the Indian Gallery. Unfortunately, many of these original portraits were destroyed in a fire at the Smithsonian Institution, where they were kept, but they survive as copies and in lithograph form. Bird returned frequently to Newport in the summer, but he died in Washington.

CAPTAIN ALBERT MARTIN (January 6, 1808–March 6, 1836) was born in Providence, the son of prominent merchant Joseph S. Martin and his wife, Abby. He received a good education, including a short stay at the U.S. Military Academy (West Point). His father's economic reverses prompted Albert, his brother and their parents to start anew around 1831 in bustling New Orleans, but by 1834 the Martins had transferred their business to Gonzales, Texas, then part of a Mexican province. When a revolt by Americans against Mexican rule erupted in 1835, Albert Martin joined the fray, becoming a captain of militia. His acts of glory and heroism came in February and March 1836 as a defender of the Alamo in San Antonio. Having left the mission-turned-fort to secure reinforcements by fighting his way out through Mexican siege lines, he then courageously returned with 32 volunteers, only to perish with them when the 187 Texan defenders fell to Santa Anna's army, estimated at nearly 3,000 men, on March 6, 1836.

CLEMENT CLARKE MOORE (July 15, 1779–July 10, 1863) was born in New York City, the son of Benjamin Moore, a well-to-do clergyman, and he graduated from Columbia University in 1798 as class valedictorian. In 1809, Moore published a highly regarded *Hebrew-English Lexicon*, and in 1821 he became professor of Greek and Hebrew at Columbia, a position he held until his retirement in 1850.

His strong ties to the Episcopal Church prompted him to donate land in Manhattan's Chatham Square that became the site for the General Theological Seminary. Despite his scholarly prominence, Moore is best remembered for his Christmas poem "A Visit from St. Nicholas," published in 1844 as part of his collected verses. He had written the poem for his six children (he eventually had nine) in 1822 while living in New York City. After retiring, Moore came permanently to Newport, residing in a twenty-five-room Victorian home still standing at 25 Catherine Street. Shortly after his death, cartoonist Thomas Nast popularized the appearance of St. Nicholas as described by Moore in his famous verses, and thus Moore and Nast, in effect, combined their talents to produce America's modern image of Santa Claus as it appeared in *Harper's Weekly* magazine, then edited by another member of the Rhode Island Heritage Hall of Fame, Providence-born George William Curtis.

SAM PATCH (1799–November 13, 1829) was born in North Reading, Massachusetts, one of six children produced by the stormy union of Samuel Greenleaf Patch and Abigail McIntire Patch. Following several family moves to northeastern Massachusetts towns, the Patches arrived in the mill village of Pawtucket at the falls of the Blackstone in 1807. Shortly after their arrival, Sam began work in Slater's "White Mill," where he rose to the coveted position of mule spinner—one of the first American-born workers to achieve this status. Sam's fame, however, would be made not in the mill but at the falls outside it: he eventually leapt feet-first from the six-story "Stone Mill" into a deep hole called "the pot," a descent of one hundred feet. In 1827, he moved to Paterson, New Jersey, where he became a boss mule spinner and leapt many times from the Clinton Bridge at Passaic Falls—a mere seventy-foot drop. By 1829, Patch—now known as the "Yankee Leaper" and the "Great Sam Patch"—had become a showman, a celebrity and one of America's first sports heroes (if one can classify height jumping as a sporting event). In October 1829, he conquered the drop next to Niagara Falls twice, but a month later he met his Waterloo at Genesee Falls in Rochester, New York. On November 6, he plunged 100 feet at the falls, but a week later, when he increased the height to 125 feet via a platform, Sam Patch jumped to his death.

COMMODORE OLIVER HAZARD PERRY (August 23, 1785–August 23, 1819) was born in South Kingstown, the son of Captain Christopher Perry, a naval officer, and Sarah Alexander, an immigrant from Ireland. He was raised in Newport and was appointed a midshipman in 1799 during the Quasi-War with France. Having served in the first war against the Barbary pirates of North Africa, he earned his immortal fame in the War of 1812 for his September 10, 1813 victory in the Battle of Lake Erie. This naval engagement prevented a British invasion of Ohio, and thus it possessed great strategic value and gave a needed boost to American morale. At the conclusion of the battle, Perry triumphantly exclaimed, "We have met the enemy, and they are ours!" In 1819, after an expedition down Venezuela's Orinoco River to open negotiations with the government of South American "liberator" Simón Bolivar, Perry contracted yellow fever and died on his thirty-fourth birthday.

COMMODORE MATTHEW CALBRAITH PERRY (April 10, 1794–March 4, 1858), the Newport-born younger brother of Oliver Hazard Perry, was a career naval officer who served in the War of 1812, the Second Barbary War against Algiers in 1815 and the Mexican War, gaining the rank of commodore in 1840. By that time, he had also earned the title the "Father of the Steam Navy" for his efforts to introduce steam power into American naval vessels. His great achievement was diplomatic in nature. In 1853 and again in 1854, his black-hulled fleet visited Japan and pressured that nation into accepting the Convention of Kanagawa, a consular treaty with the Empire of Japan, giving the United States access to the ports of Hakodate and Shimoda and opening the feudal nation to Western influence. Perry was praised and rewarded by Congress for this feat, and he prepared a valuable three-volume report on his expedition prior to his death in 1858. Both he and his famous brother are now interred in Newport's Island Cemetery. The Japan-America Society of Rhode Island holds an annual Black Ships Festival to commemorate Matthew Perry's achievement.

U.S. MINISTER AND CONGRESSMAN JONATHAN RUSSELL (February 27, 1771–February 17, 1832) was born in Providence and graduated in 1791 from Brown University. After several years in the mercantile business, he was appointed by President James Madison as American diplomatic chargé d'affaires in Paris in 1811 and then the chargé in London, a position he held when the War of 1812 began. Russell was one of the five American commissioners who negotiated the Treaty of Ghent, which ended the conflict; he did so while also serving as U.S. minister to Sweden from 1814 to 1818. Upon his return to America, he settled in Mendon, Massachusetts, and secured election to Congress in 1821. Despite serving only one term, Russell was selected the chairman of the House Committee on Foreign Affairs based on his European experiences. He died in Milton, Massachusetts, and was interred there in the family plot on his estate.

GILBERT STUART (b. Stewart, December 3, 1755–July 9, 1828) was born in South Kingstown, the son of Elizabeth Anthony and Gilbert Stewart, a Scottish immigrant who ran a snuff mill. The future artist moved to Newport at the age of six, and at age sixteen he began travels that took him to England and Ireland, then to New York and Philadelphia and eventually to Boston, where he lived and worked from 1805 until his death. Becoming one of America's foremost portraitists, he produced likenesses of over one thousand people during his prolific career, including the first six presidents. His most famous painting is an unfinished portrait of George Washington that has appeared on the dollar bill for more than a century. A number of his works were completed by his daughter, Jane Stuart (also a member of the Rhode Island Hall of Fame). He died in Boston at the age of seventy-two and is buried there in the Old South Burial Ground.

JUDAH TOURO (June 16, 1775–January 13, 1854) was born in Newport, the son of Isaac Touro, the noted rabbi of the Sephardic Jewish congregation there. With his family displaced from Newport by the British occupation during the American Revolution, in 1802 Judah ended up in New Orleans, where he became a prosperous merchant and real estate baron, known for his great philanthropy to Jewish and non-Jewish causes. In Rhode Island, his bequests included $40,000 to preserve the Jewish Cemetery in Newport and a donation to the town of the area surrounding the Old Stone Mill, a gift that is now called Touro Park. At his death, Judah Touro's bequests provided endowments for most of the Jewish congregations in the United States, as well as money for hospitals, orphanages and other charitable agencies. This very private and solitary man died in New Orleans and, fittingly, is buried in Newport's Jewish cemetery.

DR. BENJAMIN WATERHOUSE (March 4, 1754–October 2, 1846) was born in Newport to Timothy Waterhouse, a chair maker, and his wife, Hannah. At age twenty-one, he left Newport to study medicine in Europe. After his return to the United States in 1782, he joined the faculty of the new Harvard Medical School as one of its first three professors. In 1801, he introduced to America a method of cowpox vaccination to prevent smallpox that had been used in England by Dr. Edward Jenner. Waterhouse made his first vaccinations on four of his own children to prove that the Englishman's procedure was safe. In 1805, he wrote a treatise on "the evil tendency of the Use of Tobacco" by young persons. Waterhouse was also an American pioneer in the study of natural history and a well-respected advocate of botanical medicine. He died in Cambridge, Massachusetts, and is buried in Mount Auburn Cemetery.

HENRY WHEATON (November 27, 1785–March 11, 1848) was born in Providence, graduated from Brown University in 1802 and practiced law in Providence until 1812, when his legal defense of the commercial policies of Jefferson and Madison prompted Democratic Republicans in New York City to offer him the editorship of the *National Advocate*, their local party newspaper. Writing forcefully and with learning on the questions of international law growing out of the War of 1812, Wheaton was considered the mouthpiece of the Madison administration during his three-year wartime tenure with the paper. He was rewarded with the post of U.S. Supreme Court reporter in 1816, and he performed that job with ability until 1827, when he embarked on a long and successful diplomatic career, ending as minister to Prussia.

Wheaton's most enduring achievement was his work as an expounder and historian of international law. His classic study *Elements of International Law* (1836) went through numerous editions and translations. Its excellence has prompted historians to rank Wheaton with John Marshall, James Kent and Joseph Story as major architects of the American legal system. He died in Dorchester, Massachusetts.

# About the Author

D r. Patrick T. Conley is president of both the Rhode Island Heritage Hall of Fame and the Heritage Harbor Museum of Rhode Island History. Dr. Conley holds an AB from Providence College, an MA and PhD from the University of Notre Dame and a JD from Suffolk University Law School. He is the author of numerous books, most of which focus directly on Rhode Island's history, as well as dozens of similarly themed scholarly articles. He has served as chairman of the Rhode Island Bicentennial Commission, chairman and founder of the Providence Heritage Commission, chairman and founder of the Rhode Island Publications Society and general editor of the Rhode Island Ethnic Heritage Pamphlet Series. In 1977, he founded the Rhode Island Heritage Commission. He was also chairman of the Rhode Island Bicentennial [of the Constitution] Foundation, chairman of the U.S. Constitution Council and founding president of the Bristol Statehouse Foundation. He is a college professor in the subjects of history and law (Providence College, Salve Regina College, Roger Williams University School of Law), frequently gives lectures, writes an editorial column for the *Providence Journal* and publishes book reviews for the *New England Quarterly*. In May 1995, Dr. Conley became one of a handful of living Rhode Islanders to be inducted into the Rhode Island Heritage Hall of Fame. Pat lives in Bristol, Rhode Island, with his wife, Gail.